THE INVINCIBLE
Vicente Quirarte

Translated by

Elvia Ardalani

MEDIO SIGLO

Las Lenguas de Babel Collection

MEXICAN POETRY IN TRANSLATION

First Printing 2018

ISBN 13: 978-0-9995119-2-3
ISBN 10: 0-9995119-2-0

Translation Editor: Victoria M. Contreras, PhD.

Cover photograph/Fotografía de portada: *Machina en el Fuerte Sinaloa* by Lucía Leyva

Cover Design/Diseño de portada: Victoria Selene Cantú

This publication was made possible with the help of the Translation Support Program (PROTRAD) dependent of Mexican cultural institutions.

Esta publicación fue realizada con el estímulo del Programa de Apoyo a la Traducción (PROTRAD) dependiente de instituciones culturales mexicanas.

www.librosmediosiglo.org
mediosigloeditorial@gmail.com

Harlingen, Texas
USA

PRINTED IN THE UNITED STATES OF AMERICA
IMPRESO EN ESTADOS UNIDOS DE AMÉRICA

To Miguel Limón Rojas and father

Il n'y a qu'un problème philosophique vraiment sérieux:
c'est le suicide. Juger que la vie vaut ou ne vaut la peine
d'être vécue, c'est répondre à la question fondamentale
de la philosophie. Le reste, si le monde a trois dimensions,
si l'esprit a neuf ou douze catégories, vient ensuite.

Albert Camus

I run to win. If I can't win, I won't run.

Harold Abrams in *Chariots of Fire*

Tout écrivain porte en son coeur un monstre qui,
semblable au ténia dans l'estomac, y dévore les
sentiments à mesure qu'ils y éclusent. Qui triomphera?
La maladie, de l'homme, ou l'homme, de la maladie?
Certes!, Il faut être un gran homme pour tenir la balance
entre son génie et son caractère. Le talent grandit. Le
coeur se dessèche. À moins d'être un colosse, á moins
d'avoir des épaules d'Hercule, on reste ou sans coeur ou
sans talent.

Honoré de Balzac

The Invincible

Vicente Quirarte

Professor Martín Quirarte

I

It is daybreak in southern Mexico City this first Sunday of January 2010. In spite of planetary imbalances, spring dominates Mexico's basin almost all year. An unblemished and unexpected cold compensates its rigors accentuating the sinuous form of the Sleeping Woman, the sober and virile cone of the Popocatepetl. Precariously dyed by the sun, the volcanoes float in the air, drawn with a well–tempered pencil. The day begins in Ciudad Universitaria. The birds sing. They did so when the magma from the bowels of the Xitle, after closing all evidence of existence, gave way to the cooling gradual uncontrollable impulse of life. The endemic opossums stretch their muscles and start their daily quest for sustenance. They move just as serpents and jaguars always have: animals of a breed that no longer sleep and through the hand of the sculptor who gave them life work as sentinels. In this day off and at this time in the morning, the University apparently breathes only through its buildings and fields, its stadium and its flags. Tomorrow it will throb with those who give it full existence.

There are several bridges in Ciudad Universitaria. For me, one is the bridge. Due to its thin steel plates, it shakes, sounds, speaks as if responding to the vigor of the steps that touch it. Today begins the year in which I will turn the age that my father had when he died. It's Sunday and the bridge is all for me. I cross it with muscles, heart and breath that still want to sound in the symphony of the world although they do not have the strength, the brightness, the flexibility of before. Now that everything is more intense. For a long time, I evaded it. More powerful than grief, the pain mitigated giving me again the conviction that bridges are born to change the time and space. Now I pass through it whenever I can, and I celebrate it flooded with students who make the present an invincible weapon.

My father was here the last moments of his life. Sitting on the edge, with a pencil in his hand. I can confirm it because my friend Carlos Pujalte coincided in the scene, not knowing that that man,

14

on a baffling site and a disconcerting attitude, was my father. A pencil in his hand. What happened to it? Who rescued it and continued using it? And the briefcase that always accompanied him as faithful squire? My father was coming from his lecture at the Department of Philosophy and Literatures and wanted to fall into his battlefield, within the limits of the University.

Carlos used to run at noon. As part of the landscape he saw a man sitting on the bridge. Suddenly he stopped seeing him. He did not see him fall, but he did see the fallen man. It helps to know that in the midst of the curious strangers who began to crowd around, the great heart of Carlos, who for natural reasons must have palpitated more than ever, accompanied that of my father, who gradually faded. And as Roberto Moreno de los Arcos, young director of the Institute of Historical Research, was the last close person who spoke to him while the jacarandas proclaimed as nowhere else in our city the impending spring, Carlos could tell me that Dad did not die instantly: he inhaled all the air anxiously. So that the unbearable life would reach its end in high notes. So that the extraordinary life would not go away.

"And I only am escaped alone to tell thee," exclaims the Ismael of Herman Melville at the end of *Moby Dick*, with words from the *Book of Job*. Not only because I was not in Mexico when the people closest to the family began to speak, with pious and well–meaning euphemism, of the accident that Professor Quirarte had suffered, I got obsessed with reconstructing every moment of his being in the world. The morning we went together to visit the site, Carlos explained to me where Dad was sitting, the branches that his body had broken, the way in which he had calculated falling so that he would not do it on a car or under its wheels. So that he would not interrupt traffic. So that he would not spoil the rhythm of third parties. So that life could continue and the sole work of his tribe was to decipher the indecipherable.

What book was he carrying? What is said to a group of students when the next act of life is going to be to end it? One of the repeat readings of my father was the story of Alphonse Daudet about a

French teacher, during the Prussian occupation of 1871, who tells his students that by orders of the invaders only the German language will be taught in the schools of Alsace and Lorena. Therefore, he has been removed from his post and that will be the last class. At the end of it, when he hears the Prussians coming back from their military exercises he writes on the board *Vive la France*. The narrative voice is articulated by a student who is late to class and had never made the most of the lessons of the teacher who for forty years went to great lengths to prove that French was the most beautiful language in the world –heritage, pride, homeland identity– because Monsieur Hamel said, "when a people fall into slavery, if they keep their own language well, it is as if they have the key to the prison."

After teaching the one that was his last class, did my father have his coat on or had he removed it to relieve the heat? I did not ask Carlos and only now the question appears. When the decisive moment arrives, regardless the disruption that accompanies the separation of the natural rhythm of life, there is an attachment to the ritual that puts prince and pauper on the same stave: the last slow and hearty breakfast of Maximilian, the final glass of wine at six in the morning, before being executed in Querétaro. The character recalled by George Orwell who, barefoot and with a loincloth, has the instinctive elegance to avoid a puddle when going to the site of his execution.

The bridges and the distressed ones. Strange, inevitable couple. The truly defeated are not saved. Lovers sometimes are. Voracious like no one, love breaks them with a dry lightning and gives them the possibility of resurrection. The others throw themselves sure to bring an anchor on the neck. Whoever evades the Grim Riper unhinges the needles of the quadrant: his time has not arrived. Only the samurai who sinks on himself his obedient steel, arrogant and bright as ever, is lord of life and death.

II

He did what all men do: ninety–nine times he entered through the exit and the hundredth got the wrong door. He tasted the bitter fruit in times of sweetness, but boarded as many trains as he encountered. For forty days he sailed aboard an Italian freighter where he learned to hate spaghetti, read pages from *Ulises Criollo* and discovered the conquest of ocean routes. He liked crud and Bordeaux wine; he received the touch of coffee with milk several times. Once it was in the middle of the cold London where he knew he was happy while someone talked to him about Thomas de Quincey and his useless search in the fog. Perhaps because he read about the charge of the Chinacos, the gun fire of April 2 in Puebla, the thunder of the cannons in Calpulalpan, his ears were deaf to music. But he loved poetry, he walked around New York and he wrote to his son Ignacio on the back of a postcard from Brooklyn Bridge about his encounter with a giant who told him: "My name is Walt and my last name is Whitman." He believed in the songs of Édith Piaf, in the novels of Flaubert, in Marilyn Monroe, in travel books, in a prostitute from the rue Blondel, in loaders and drunkards from the Lagunilla neighborhood that promised him: "For sure I will pay you tomorrow." One night, in a restaurant in Saint–Denis he dined with a veteran of the Second World War: he was thinking of another battlefield; the white page little by little populated with buildings, windows, corridors. With the first amphetamine of the day he knew that while love sometimes deceives us, the light never betrays those who seek it. He thought – when his ghosts would not arrive punctually – that a blank page is a body willing to surrender, a boat about to be assaulted, a shot of cognac in the rain. He accompanied his heroes in fights without objectives. Aboard his time machine, he traveled through all the ages and spaces. He did what all men do. *He wrote, loved, lived.*

To warm up the hand and cool the heart, I write this portrait of Professor Martín Quirarte. Of the father who formed me in the first quarter of a century of my life I have left testimony in poems where I allow myself to unleash the emotion that he restrained in us. I invoke him and it seems I see him with his hurried walk, his Bostonian shoes, his shirt which was not always the one of a happy man. When it was, there was no monarch who could buy it. I hear him laughing at a Bourvil film, with spontaneity and childlike scandal. I reconstruct his daily literal journey through Mexico's history, when the world was the downtown streets, from the door of the old San Ildefonso College to our house on Allende Street; I smell him in the careful underlining of his books, in his deserted suits. I perceive him in my blood, in my huge fears. In my stubbornness to consummate small victories over the world.

His students and friends know, better than I do, that his rigor in the everyday classroom or in the leap of faith called an exam was his way of loving. Writing a thesis under his direction was a torment, the assurance that the tortured one had done a more solid work than the caravels, both in the exposed arguments as in how words are combined to say what we really wanted to. In love with the impeccable construction, with the fair word that kept Flaubert awake, he wanted the facts to be emptied in bronze molds, not in crumbling plaster constructions collapsing with the passing of time. His students at the Patria Institute knew him by the nickname "El Esperado" because he was so distracted that cheating on his test was more than a challenge an invitation. But in the oral exam it was a different issue and a different way of a teacher demonstrating devotion to his students. He forced all of them to learn, he advised all of them to have a Sancho to keep their Quixote. He was the first to disregard his own advice. His initial book is, almost, a manifesto of life: *Carlos Pereyra, Caballero Andante de la Historia* (Carlos Pereyra, Errant Knight of History).

Our Department of Philosophy and Literature awards degrees whose justice is not impartial. No graduate of Philosophy with self–respect will say he is a philosopher, nor a graduate from Literature will boast that he is a man of letters. In contrast, a person who studies history is called a historian. Martín Quirarte did not consider himself a historian, but a promoter of history. He never forgot his initial occupation was saddlery, a trade inherited from generations of Quirartes in the San Juan de Dios market in Guadalajara. Thus, his work desk did not forget the order and symmetry of the saddler's workshop. One of his great lessons was that writing is such a solitary work, such a thankless job, that it is necessary to surround yourself with the greatest amount of toys that help you to forget that ungratefulness. He loved the freshly sharpened pencils, the fountain pens always loaded with ink of a color that may well be called *martinian*. He wrote his drafts in very fine paper, whose spending was justified by saying that he spent on cigarettes. Chaotic child, obsessed with order, he designed his own furniture, and always had more books than bookcases. Henri Pirenne, one of his favorite authors, defined the historian as a man who loves life and knows how to contemplate it. Martín Quirarte loved life and history with this joyful fatality. Similar to the bad actors that before transmitting emotion let themselves be won by emotion, he was unable to conjure up some epic page without a trembling voice. More than an historian, he was a poet of history. More than an intellectual, he was a worker who built his paragraphs with the same care with which he assembled the pieces of a charro chair. But if he was at work, he was organized and methodical, in the acts of daily life he carried the lost compass of the wise. Two–legged animal who never learned to drive, he often left home without money. When he realized it, since borrowing money was a humiliation, he preferred to cover the journey walking. Sometimes, when I met him in the corridors of the National Preparatory School or in the Department, I would greet him, he would address me formally, saying "nice to meet you" and would follow along, while continuing in his monologue. I am lying. He actually spoke to Cyrano de Bergerac or to Jean–Baptiste Pocquelin.

From Justo Sierra he learned the conceptual strength and the narrative sense of history; from Martín Luis Guzmán, the secrets of punctuation; from Francisco Alonso Bulnes and Carlos Pereyra, the polemical spirit. Enemy of party hatreds, Martín Quirarte believed in equity and justice. That is how he could write a book like *El Problema Religioso en México* (The Religious Problem in Mexico), which won praise from both, diehard clericals and Archbishop Sergio Méndez Arceo. In his studies of the Reformation and the French Intervention, his conciliatory work became apparent again. He insisted on reading and analyzing the interventionists, the monarchists and the clericals, he became a lawyer for the vanquished and taught us, as he learned from his teacher José C. Valadés, to know them rather than condemn them without appeal. In 1970 appeared the one that is perhaps his greatest work: *Historiografía sobre el Imperio de Maximiliano* (Historiography on Maximilian's

Empire). Its prelude is formed by the words from another of his teachers, Agustín Yáñez:

> It is not the time to revive liquidated passions, nor to incur in sterile grudges; but it's time to review the centennial lesson to avoid past mistakes and verify the paths to follow.

Poor but delicate, unable to bear the humiliation of our doubly medieval libraries, Martín Quirarte turned to obtain bibliographical material necessary to carry out his work in original editions. Around payday, used booksellers from Lagunilla would hang around our house depriving us of the scarce income of the month. In return, they provided us with books that were candidates to enter the Monte de Piedad non-profit pawnshop. My brothers and I don't forget the day he sent us to pawn the first edition of *Mexico: Su Evolución Social.* If we ever had doubts about the weight of the Porfiriato regime, hauling the heavy books to Montepío convinced us of that irrefutable historical truth. He also used to quote the phrase from Vasconcelos that an unbound book is not a book. Since he never had enough money to bind all his volumes, he devised an effective method:

taking two or three more or less the same size copies, even if they were of different subjects, and bind them in one volume. I kept one of them with *The Little Prince* of Antoine de Saint–Exupéry and the *Santa Anna* of Rafael F. Muñoz. When I told José Emilio Pacheco he replied that more than a coincidence, it was a historical judgment from my father. Poor seller of the works that he bought at exorbitant prices, at his death he left in the bank only the amount of the sale of a first edition in four volumes of Rousseau's *Emile,* that served completely to pay his funeral.

Professor Quirarte always looked for the closeness of the young, and never forgot the High School where he was formed. He loved it so much that not only did he teach there throughout his academic life, but he also wrote the history of it in an exemplary book because of its sense of synthesis and interpretation, entitled *Gabino Barreda, Justo Sierra y el Ateneo de la Juventud* (Gabino Barreda, Justo Sierra and the Athenaeum of Youth). Like all teenagers, I too was ashamed of my father. I remember, specially, my classmates 'mockery when they visited my home. Once when I was distracted, my father took them to his workroom to share with them the beautiful Fernand Braudel's theory upon which the book rebels. Once we have written it, it no longer belongs to us and we must, as we do with a child, let it go. The following days, my friends kept saying, "this guy's dad says the book reveals itself." In the deliberate linguistic confusion of my friends there is another one of Martín Quirarte's lessons: as the artist that he was he believed in revelation, he fixed that rapture in writing and afterwards accepted the rebellion of the book that, once autonomous, took its own way.

To that momentary shame followed the satisfaction that Martín Quirarte became a friend of my friends, and they would look for him even when I was not around. I start reminiscing and I find them each of them in a different communication channel. I evoke Miguel García Colorado and my father, both with their eyes closed in trance and running their hands over a German edition of anthological photos of Marilyn Monroe; I see him walking the streets of downtown next to Sergio López Mena, his only squire who shared his taste for Burger Boy, places so inhospitable that nobody wanted to spend more than fifteen minutes there and were, therefore, the best spaces to work. It grieves me to see his disgust at the excesses of my brother José Francisco Ortega and later, to be faithful to the historical image of the Acatempan embrace, the reconciliation without any other word, except for the understanding of friendship. I hear him getting into the catchy music of the San Luis Club along with Roberto Morales, looking for the redemption of the underworld. I catch him at a downtown *taquería* or at a bar in a cantina, celebrating the fresh puns of Jesús Franco; I envy him holding arms with Elia Espinosa, my teenage girlfriend whose sentimental education my father was charged with, due to the inexperience of his son, and to better understand the teacher's lesson.

I said before that Martín Quirarte was a poet of history. I wish that statement was not understood as an elegant metaphor but as a reality. Elia Espinosa's book on Jean Cocteau opens with the following inscription: "In memory of Don Martín

Quirarte, historian, poet in life itself, misunderstood." There is the triple condition as historian, poet and a misunderstood person, words that in the case of Professor Quirarte are synonymous. He who dreamed of having decent children, professionals with successful careers as good people have, engineers or accountants, was my first poetry teacher. Not only of the poetry of life, in that he was the best of my teachers; I am referring more to the poetry of the verb. He, who considered himself hopeless for music, taught it to me in the poetry of Baudelaire. The first poem I learned by heart, without knowing what it meant, was "Un hemisphère dans un chevelure", not for any other reason, but because my father would repeat it enjoying its cadence, sensually repeating the words of that poem where Baudelaire transformed the thick hair of Jeanne Duval in a gateway to other worlds. Juan González, his brother of philological passions, evokes the enthusiasm with which he transcribed and recorded *Andromaque*, especially because he was interested in the girl playing the female role. In the name of that love for the French language, he published a notebook with the popular songs of the fifties.

He found his happiness in his work, in the creation of worlds. His plans for future research were vast, excessive, impossible. He worked beyond the capacity of his strength. The ghosts that his blood gave life to, defeated him. The amphetamines, that truck drivers ingest to drill the night and fog, were the vampires who elevated him and destroyed him on his long nocturnal journeys. Young Martín started taking them at a very early age as a stimulus to study, build, dream with his eyes open. He could not recuperate from the workloads that he forced himself to in 1972, during the death anniversary of Benito Juárez. In addition to preparing the best editions of classic works on the Reform and the Intervention, that year he published what would be his last book: *Las Relaciones entre Juárez y el Congreso* (The Relations between Juárez and Congress). Then came the collapse, the admission to psychiatric hospitals, and the conviction that nothing would be the same. There his level headedness, his Christian spirit, his ability to laugh and make people laugh were tested, regardless of the big black sun that he had in place of a heart.

In poetry, ahead of action, lies the last exemplary lesson of Professor Martín Quirarte, when he turned away completely from this existence and its minor worries. I remain convinced that he died like the heroes die, like so many characters who paraded before his eyes. Those who did not love him and saw in his death the end of rage, translated that act as a natural byproduct of the deep and intermittent depression that he suffered during his last years. Those of us who knew him and loved him, soon realized that his farewell was a supreme gallantry toward the living and the only lesson a teacher can give us: to move aside to make way for those coming behind us. The bridge where he died thus becomes a parable, a poetic image and a moral lesson. Bridges were made to unite people, to overcome obstacles. The life and work of Martín Quirarte were dedicated to erect bridges. When he felt that he could no longer build them, he chose one of them to end his earthly adventure. Luis Cernuda, whom I then read with a devotion that over the years has accentuated, gave me a possible answer: "Dying is hard, but not being able to die if everything dies is perhaps harder." Professor Martín Quirarte did not want a tomb or a monument. He does not have a classroom with his name in the department where he taught. But that bridge remains as a testimony to the integrity of his passing on Earth.

III

I write these words more than twenty years after
making the previous portrait. I endorse them now. I
made them for the one who was my teacher, first in
time, "in loving fire, all burning." I talked about him,
not about what has been dying in me ever
since. Then came the time of restless rebels; I see
myself in his falls, in his weaknesses that I repeat
though I daringly fight against them. In my family,
I am the one who physically looks more like him, the
closer heir to his phobias, but also to his love of
harmony that eventually left him. I think I even
owe him "the habit heroically insane of talking to
oneself." His selfless heroism, his final courage, his
beautifully tragic aura defended me at first from the
thin and sharp pain that apparently was not
willing to leave. However, I was never so exposed to
beauty. I would sit at a fountain in Independencia
Street to kill time before going to teach orthography
to secretaries and policemen from the Bank of

Mexico, because after the death of my father I had to accept all the additional jobs that would come up.

The fountain had and has now, recently restored, a female sculpture that accompanied and comforted me. I would look at it and admire it as if it were the first time. Twice necessary and worthy of gratitude was also the beauty of the secretaries, their natural and unconscious freshness that relieved all wrong. Pain set aside those we used to call pains. It refined life with capital letters. The relentless appetite of death accentuated the hue of each note that had been there from the beginning but never before understood. As if I had to breathe multiple times the air that was left as my inheritance. Besides, I was in the lighted doorway of love as I had not known it before and that fullness faced, invincible, the jaws of the shadow.

The fall of the guardian trunk marked our life with white stone. Still warm the ashes that were delivered to us after cremation, I became my father's heir. I was in such a natural way, as my mother and my four brothers, but I became obsessed with rebuilding his ways, wading through the quicksand that lost him, trying to solve the complex maze of his passions.

The letter that Dad left for us states as the only explanation of his voluntary death that it has been some time since he cannot write. I do not know where I keep it. I do not know if I have it. Therefore I cannot confirm now if he wrote "difficulty writing" or "inability to write." It's the same for the one receiving as the main inheritance choosing between writing or death as the only options of combat. His zeal for life had been extinguished and could make his the words of Kurt Cobain: "I don't have the passion anymore, and so remember, it's better to burn out than to fade away" whose second part Bernardo Esquinca took to impeccable hendecasyllable verses: " Es mejor incendiarse que borrarse" (It is better to burn than being erased). Dad wrote a letter to be read by his family, but he never talks for a moment about us. The suicide victim is the biggest egomaniac, but also the most justified: after overcoming all fears he finds that existence is absurd and does not recognize the mediocre reward of daily life anymore. Each new

37

page is more difficult, and more so the anguish when you think it's time to remain silent. In the first instance, there is a contradiction. When one is truly a writer and one gets to know the secrets of the trade, the distance between what is thought and what is written is shortened, as the lightning of discovery and its rendition to the page or typewriter, between the sudden metaphor that claims its vigorous birth and its transformation into words that violate the flexible armor of language. Downfall comes from feeling that the armor is invincible. More exactly, when one knows that combat is useless. A strategy: to recognize the moment when, if we have nothing to say, we are willing to accept other forms, not necessarily undignified, of existing. Or if the time has come to erase ourselves completely.

The image of the bear appeared in an untimely way in the first poems I wrote, coinciding with the decline of Dad. His eldest and unreachable brother was *The Tiger in the House* by Eduardo Lizalde, one of the books that contributed the most to my elementary education in the school of the authentic accursed poets. My creature, the bear, flaunted the letters of its name, but at the same time it was transfigured into a wall that closed the original impulses leaving me in a bramble bristling with nameless edges. It is possible that we will encounter the bear when we least expect it or that when the meeting happens we don't have weapons nor the ability to beat it. Running away is valid. We believe we let it go when in reality he –or she or that –is the one who frees us. Or it imposes its unbearable weight.

The creation process is interrupted, it detours. Or it gets perverted and becomes frustrated. To create is to breathe and not to create is to die. To create is to live and to stop doing it is a death longer than death. The ultimate betrayal of Narcissus, but absolute loyalty to what we are deeper. The need for life to be integrated in such a high intensity that it risks not happening again. Fyodor Dostoevsky tried to write a pamphlet against alcoholism and the result was the great anatomy of human behavior entitled *Crime and Punishment.* The obligation of every artist required by Cyril Connolly can be a line, an image, a moment, even if to reach them we navigate in a sea of silence, of continuous defeats.

When I was a child, my grandmother told me that if I looked at myself too much in the mirror, the devil would appear to me. The phrase is full of wisdom and symbols, but in those years it was for me the most terrible of curses. The writer is the most solitary of beings and therefore the most exposed to summon the devil. The natural resource, biophilic, is the creation that exorcises and purifies, even if it touches the most despicable and corrupt. That one who cannot be alone with himself should not try to write. I cannot spend too much time with myself, but when I have accomplished that prodigious split I have found an unprecedented form of happiness. "I fight with myself. Defend me God against myself." Cristóbal de Castilleja's verse, revealed by the wisdom of my professor Antonio Alatorre, synthesizes this condition and its successive transformations in that other that lives within us, and that I have strenuously searched for both in my readings as in my own experience.

"Never offer the bear's skin before having killed it," popular wisdom dictates. In other words, do not say what you're going to do before you do it. The territory for hunting is different in each of its daring practitioners. Equally is its time. There are closed seasons, but never for the one who faces only the impossible reoccurring adventure. The best reward for an artist, said Baudelaire, is taking to the field of execution what he imagined from the beginning. For those who blindly believe in the great master of objectivity, the conscious poet who did not keep out hallucination nor surprise, his idea is a dogma. To follow it as an emblem brings with it whiteness, emptiness. The nothingness that annihilates, not that which leads to wise silence. Over time you learn that the apparent emptiness of the paper, that whiteness of the ungraspable, ubiquitous Moby Dick, is a lure for laziness and a mirror of its no less dangerous sister that we sometimes write with capital letters: death. *La Mujerte* (The Womandeath,) as Francisco Sánchez named it. When the imagined is not transferred to the page with the intensity and passion with which we feel they are born, the only solution is to continue trying. The words of T.S. Eliot pose an answer and a relief, but also a new requirement: "And so each venture is a new beginning / a raid in the inarticulate."

Like other dreamers who believe that in order to write one must enter a school of letters, in 1973 I registered in the Department of Philosophy and Letters, majoring in Hispanic Language and Literatures. My decision was due to two reasons: the first one, a refusal to study architecture, the only career that according to my father and his only brother was going to guarantee my happiness; the second one, the full conviction that the best writer in Mexico crossed the threshold of the University. Small was the court for the victory, tiny the plain for my horse to run wild. Fortunately, from the beginning I faced great trainers that made me learn the hard way that every verbal adventure is the first one. I had the privilege of having Eduardo Lizalde and Salvador Elizondo as my professors —my teachers— and they never had mercy for the texts that I began to write. Hernán Lavín Cerda, who had just arrived from Chile, introduced us into a universe of personal and collective reminiscences, through his sweet and generous voice. To Lizalde and Elizondo I also owe the conviction that has never left me that writing is an impossible task that one does because there is no choice. What may sound like false modesty is actually the best defense I've had when I feel that a text is finished. The only consolation left to an active writer is that his next job will always be the best.

I have never regretted having entered a department where I am now a professor, I obtained my PhD and I have only received satisfaction from it. Another great lesson from Spider Man: Peter Parker enters college because he does not want to spend all his life selling pictures to *The Daily Bugle*, the same way although I did not consider unworthy working as a test grader or teaching classes to indifferent high school students, I wanted to fully exercise the powers which I had been initiated for. The University seemed, in this sense, the best battlefield. Because of the different expectations and the dysfunction that we all face when starting late to do what we most love, and then as now I know that young writers who continue to enter it, have every right and reason in the world when they express the worst epithets to that ungrateful and demanding stepmother, that is not but one of many branches of Life, that profession that we never learn well enough. Ernesto Sábato, paraphrasing Emerson, says that the real writer is born in the street and not in a literature department. Precisely, Sábato's first fiction book, *The Tunnel*, was my decisive companion of those difficult months when life is demanding and you cannot deal with it. A few months after entering the Department where I thought everything would be happiness, I received an extended visit from Our Lady Melancholy, once called black bile, a wedge, noonday demon. It was a more powerful and deadly enemy than the villains Peter Parker faced. I would wake up with the realization that it stood at the foot of my bed, with its harpy wings and its gorgon head. I reread and lived the most distressing poems by Neruda in *Residence on Earth*; another *Tiger in the house* was watching beneath my pillow; I searched myself in the existential helplessness of Rafael Alberti's *Concerning the Angels*, undertook long solitary walks under the rain on the French Cemetery of the Mercy. I didn't tell anyone what was happening, because the effect of my illness was not noticeable in my flesh; I just knew –without knowing– that I was unable to control the beast, that my hunger had awakened. Sábato's *The Tunnel*, perhaps the book that I emphasized the most those years, reaffirmed in me the idea of being different, fighting with the world.

One good day in April 1977 –how could I not remember– while the jacarandas were blooming everywhere in Mexico City, I found myself cured, ready to live the life in which I had spent four years as if in the dark. That spring I fell in love and started a navigation that lasted more than twenty years, which domesticated my beast without killing it. Naturally, the visits from the dark angel continue –without notice and without knocking on the door– in my life. Popular wisdom claims that God does not send difficult tasks for fools and Neo Platonists discovered that thinking beings live under the power of Saturn, the Astro of Melancholy, but time has taught me that the fullness of life is not at odds with creation.

"What time do you write?" Statement rather than question. He who questions perceives us victims of the enemies of the writer, those big trifles consuming the energy that we would only want dedicated to the struggle with the interior antagonist that does not forgive. More than enemies of the writer they are enemies of writing, because the one who has managed to translate his passions into verbal objects capable of withstanding the passage of the years can live without writing. Can one be a writer without writing? Yes, when it has been discovered that writing is one of the highest tasks in the world. But also one of the most exhausting, thankless, frustrating; and almost always impossible. The real writer writes what he must. He is silent when he should be. Juan Rulfo and Alí Chumacero knew it. However, until we can breathe the transparency of those summits, we must continue trying.

It is possible to respond with calculated intelligence, although our inquisitor realizes that we do it with the best mask and a bunch of platitudes. It is possible to invoke the lack of time and other allies. The greatest enemy is articulated in first person, the self that is another and expects of us what vanity and common sense try to avoid at all costs. For love, as for writing, there is always time, but the second occupation is more demanding and absorbent. The mastery of technique is not enough. The word goes with he who better serves it, who feels it better. With the one who resists the most.

When I sensed that my main occupation would be writing, I tried to do what I thought I had seen in my models: to devote myself entirely to literature not thinking about anything else. *La vraie vie est absente*, I read in Rimbaud and I labored to transform the phrase into dogma. Fortunately, I can count the times I have shut myself out with the sole desire to write. The result has been as sterile as dramatic, as pathetic as unfruitful. In that attitude I find, also, a bad example of Dad: he took a plane to Acapulco and in his suitcase he carried a couple of shirts and bunch of insurgent books. He would return defeated twice, not having rested nor having written the page he expected. In contrast to that masochistic attitude, gradually I learned in a natural way, fortunately for me and the family with whom I share this terrestrial adventure, that in the search for words they swell, and are organized into syntactical groups, the exercise of life goes on and leads, inevitably, to a place where the written form corresponds to it in a better way, although in appearance it is further away from it.

With humiliation at the beginning, with humility later, I have accepted that for me writing is being the shortest continuous time with my demon. That is why it is similar to the activity of a child when doing homework and interrupting it continuously because he has to go kick the ball, open the refrigerator door without taking anything, hoping that they knock at the door because the trash can must be emptied. Interruptions are blessings because writing –for me– is an impossible task that gives its true fruits only occasionally. However, we shall always abhor that who with the best intentions tells us, as the poet remembers: "Come to dinner, wild one, the milk is hot."

You can live without writing, but if previously there has been a real relationship with writing, in the same way that you can live without love after having lived with the frenzy and dedication it deserves. He who decides to stop writing and enjoy those intensities in a different way is a genuine master. The how I write inevitably ends in the where, word that has the double meaning of support and space. A notebook and a coffee are the best passport to paradise, the best battle station to write drafts, sieges. Skirmishes. Then comes the final, real battle, where losing —and accepting we lose— is an alternate form of honor. That little notebook, that stoic assistant, accepts our incisions and holds for instants the brightness and weight of the ink. The notebook gives structure and dispels chaos. And a coffee shop, preferably where no one knows us, or we become so familiar that we achieve the silence of a chair. A coffee shop where it is possible to be alone in a crowd, and yet accompanied by it. A coffee that is ours as Tomás Segovia made El Comercial de

Madrid his, and whose small careful handwriting built vast universes every morning, enlightening us with its white moral light.

Martin Eden, the autobiographical character in Jack London's namesake novel, decides to end his life when he repeats to himself over and over again, in the increasing success and financial rewards of his writings: "All that I am now I already was before." Relative truth. Beyond the fame and its ghosts the writer is waiting for his true readers, or for that only reader who will understand what the other's words meant. "Thank you for this book that taught me to live" is one of the dedications that with more pleasure I remembered from Eliseo Diego. And another one of my professors, César Rodríguez Chicharro, who after the suicide of my father told me satirically disguising his inclination to tragedy, that my father had betrayed us all, for he, too, most of the time felt frustrated because his printed words did not even approach what he had conceived. In exchange there were many other possibilities of extending the talents that, in one way or another, we have been granted: teaching, friendship, fierce joy. One night, while returning from one of the memorable dinners with Rodríguez Chicharro at the Hipódromo restaurant anchored forever in the middle of the past century, followed by a night walk with the professor, I got to my house, hugging an ostentatious copy of the complete works of César Vallejo given to me by the other César. During one of his stays in the United States as a visiting professor, he had done what he never did in his life: a journal of his readings. He did not write what he knew in his opinion was not worth it, but the log of the wild reader who becomes dignified when he really is already. The reader as an artist, a relentless fighter of the Narcissus who lives lurking in every creator. As it was my friend Álvaro Rendón. "Did you see Feroz already?" They asked me in one of my beneficial returns to Culiacán, love to which the constant aura of Gilberto Owen leads me. They suppressed the article, because the adjective, naturally with capital letter, was the true name, the heteronomous of Álvaro Rendón. Those who questioned me had been inoculated by that uncompromising passion that the professor would put in in what he lived reading, in what he read living. His question had numerous nuances. I had not yet seen Feroz, but seeing him was a fiesta and a necessity. What was imperative for him, and his friends too, was talking about books, authors, the arts. Never to talk bad about the person who had procreated them. It was the last reader of Ricardo Piglia. That's why it was the first. Someone born to love and build, to dream and to rebel through books. Knowledge was not what we most admired in him, but his enthusiasm. The way his eyes sparkled when invoking what had dazzled him and taught him not to understand, but to live. To live with sweat and joy, furies and sorrows that real literature provides. What it taught us, without saying, was that we are the sum of the readings that inevitably find us, those that wallow us, sink us and save us. When the reader has the double good fortune to become a writer, he erases the seams and leaves us facing the creature that could be conceived.

One day I asked him: « Why do they call you Feroz?" And with that childlike spontaneity, so like him, he explained: "My brother was nicknamed

Handsome and since it was necessary to give me a nickname, the only thing that occurred to them was the opposite, that is, *Ugly*. To soften it, it was changed to *Ferocious* ". I remembered the dialogue of Jesús Inclán in *The Forgotten Ones* when he tells a child. "What a lame nickname you have." And if Alvaro's was so at first, time showed us that some names are defined by opposition: Feroz was meek as true brave people are.

César Ibarra, from Culiacán, sent me an email, laconic and terrible, "They shot Feroz dead." Impeccable pentameter, worthy of a song dedicated to those who are killed with the iron that they wielded too. Then I got details from Ignacio Trejo: He was coming from visiting César López Cuadras, also from Sinaloa, a writer who also puts the literature discourse above the weapons discourse. What makes Feroz different in death? What makes him so close to us? Every day, and it is not a hyperbole, we are killed by what is dearly ours in a constantly more mutilated territory. Death puts the forced nomad and the university professor at the same level. The bells are ringing for all. However, we

could not reproach Álvaro for being sort of a
scoundrel. How noble he was that even alcohol was
not handled well by him. It made him more eloquent
and enthusiastic, more generous and childish. He
was an oasis in the vast and small territory,
generous and mean spirited of our Literary
Republic. Talking to him made us less despicable.

Feroz would have been the first to demand resorting
to the heroism of humor that our professor Alí
Chumacero taught us. At eighty years of age when
he was asked what else he needed in life, he replied
laconically, solemnly and mischievously: "Being
stabbed by a jealous husband." Feroz lacked being
shot to death, and not dying of pains and undignified
moods in a hospital bed. I am sure that, as a man of
honor, he gave no sign of weakness. I hope he was
granted, as the character of Élmer Mendoza in
Trancapalanca –which really is him, in one of his
encounters with Death– having said in the coward's
face that in that moment dominated the thread
between life and death: "Pull it, Sir." And addressing
the murderer formally, to make his vileness more
distant.

IV

*Will there be another way of writing that is
not pushed into it by a need
stronger than desire for silence?*

Frédéric–Yves Jeannet,
Light of the World

Writing is a leading act. Preliminary private acts
that take place when exercising the loneliest of
trades perhaps will never leave the four walls the
writer has chosen as a prison for his conditional
freedom –parole– or may become writings claiming
their autonomy: Flaubert's letters describing his
suffering to give life to Madame Bovary are an
example of the transformation of the object of
writing in an active subject of knowledge. My father
turned to them consistently, as a necessary
unavoidable medicine is used.

In what moment does such a leading action
become antagonistic and convert the writer and the
writing no longer tacit subjects into the main
elements of the work? The writer is the creator of
worlds, whose validity depends on their autonomy

and authenticity. In the real writer, the self becomes the "we"

who baptizes and initiates the one responsible for having created that universe. But there comes a moment when the writer needs to be heard not from his finished works but from the dark areas where he creates his texts, from those invisible scaffoldings, unexpected when the text no longer allows to contemplate its cracks nor the tools that served for the task.

The first modern novel is a reflection on the writer and writing. His author managed to establish a double dimension of reading to create the image of the hypothetical writer who said what the actual one established in writing. Cervantes writes long after the ancient ones established the dramatic *Nihil sub sole novum*. That is how it was discovered by the one from Lepanto when submerging in the mighty river of chivalric romances. When writing a new one, he reclaims and transforms the genre, but takes writing to a dead end: we can only write about what has been said. Between *Don Quixote* and James Joyce's *Ulysses*, between Góngora's poetry and

Finnegan's Wake there are three centuries of combat between language and its perpetrator. Hence, as the scriptural activity is transformed and becomes more complex, the work and its relationship to life, the task of the writer, the occult mechanisms behind the work become the writer's obsession who writes because he must. *Escribir sin para qué* is the title, ironic and dramatic, from a book by Ángel José Fernández, while Eduardo Hurtado concludes:

> *Here I am: I have my trade;*
> *Stationmaster*
> *No whistle and no fixed schedule*
> *With continuous running*
> *To the fear of the desert.*

To such approach, the answer would be writing just because, since failure to do so, would be a catastrophe similar to the biological one, and such termination of literary activity would lead to death. The character of the short story by Julio Cortázar "Letter to a Young Lady in Paris" is a birthing of life: the bunnies that he gives life to are the creatures the writer cannot control. Once he feels unable to live with them, he has no other choice than death.

Futility as a form of death is a phenomenon of our modernity; at least a phenomenon that our modernity makes tangible and recurring. The light of reason was not enough to annihilate the Renaissance specter of acedia, that form of death that is the inability to create, to escape that enclosure. Writing is creating life; not doing it is to kill the vital impulse that gave birth to what all men live but only the writer is able to rescue, select and translate. For the man endowed with the ability to write, filling out a sheet with the signs of the tribe is an ethical obligation that leads him to fidelity to an aesthetic. Life and its impulses are ethical elements, roads towards victory and the continuation of the species, expressed at its highest marks. However, when that initial flight is interrupted, the writer does not only live his ghosts but is forced to make his task the subject of writing itself: *Why do I write? How do I write?*

In the eighteenth century literary precepts, poetics became a set of technical rules: reason ordered chaos, weeded the jungle fertilized by the baroque imagination. Like Hoffmann's androids, the

writer was a reasoning machine, a tracker of
passions. Voltaire, Laclos and Sade are an example
of this objective anatomy of the body and heart.
Since Romanticism, the writer is a character acting
not only on paper but in the wider scenario of
history. To the ancient warrior societies, the writer
was one more of his trade; for industrialized
societies, the writer is "the wrong conscience of his
time", warns Saint–John Perse. Romanticism was
the great discovery of the first person. Novels and
poems manifest from their titles, the importance of
the name, the fundamental task of the protagonist.
Romantic heroes are sensible, creators, adventurers
who translate what they are, like Byron, or
whatever they wanted to be, as Walter Scott. In
Mexico, Ignacio Manuel Altamirano masquerades
under another name in the novel *Clemencia*, where
the interplay between history and fiction, as well as
concern for style, make this work the first artistic
novel in our literature. Writer and medical doctor
Juan Díaz Covarrubias barely disguises himself in
his poet and doctor characters, young professionals
determined to tear down, with the lights of their

knowledge, a three–time secular regime. More than worried, engaged in the deciphering of the self, the characters are the writers, and do not need to question their task as such. Prior to the ivory tower that Alfred de Vigny will build once the revolutionary disappointment invades the writers, our Romantics occupy the trench, the government office, the speaker's stand. Their literature has a utilitarian character, a battle weapon whose need is unquestionable.

The apparent truce between the writer and the writing breaks when a teenager traces in the barn of the family home in Roche, in northern France, a chilling phrase: "I *is* another" For the Romantic dogma, Arthur Rimbaud's assertion sounded like heresy. However, the declaration is a manifest and an extension of Romanticism that had begun exploring the fathomless depths of the soul, the immersion into the unknown to find the new, the disarray of all the senses. In that meteor of increasing intensity starting with Nerval, passing through Baudelaire and Rimbaud, one of the explanations of modernity is found: submersion is necessary, although in the return to light there is nothing left to say. Someone else writes for me while I live and love and enjoy and suffer and die. The genesis of such division was in the confrontation of the Romantics. If for some of them the art joined together the characteristics of beauty and advised usefulness, for others it was more transcendent than the writing self was an autonomous being who listened to outside voices. Stéphane Mallarmé will discover what had always been there, but that modernity reveals in all its helplessness and greatness: the blank page as a judgment against a sterile rhetoric. From this point of view, mallarmenian whiteness is a praise of potential poetry, of latent writing and of that to come. Silence is not so much futility but an awareness that words do not say what vision guesses.

The performance of the writer in the work increases to the extent that such characteristics— ironically always undefined— of the creature are define that when created by us lends itself to be a lightning rod in the storm and is articulated through language coherence. It is no coincidence that during

Romanticism, the issue of the double, the *doppelgänger*, acquires a full naturalization letter, one of whose main aspects is that of the writer who comes to life, either from the fantastic point of view or from the symbolic one. In the novel *Mist*, Miguel de Unamuno explores the uncertain boundaries between the creator and his work. Guillermo Samperio, in his text *She Lived in a Short–Story* further complicates this game between protagonist, writer and subject, to the point that the combination results in a third language: that of writing, in constant crosslinking with the reality lived by the author and the reality built in the body of the story.

The Romantic split acquires particular characteristics in the case of Latin–American authors. From the moment they are born to a new republic, they accept an unprecedented identity. In the new republics, born in the aftermath of the first Great Revolution, the writers do not have time to meditate on the metaphysics of their task: the urgencies of the moment lead them to change the pen for the sword, the office for the parliamentarian stand or the public plaza; their writing is eminently utilitarian in character, confronting reality directly. If every writer fights against an enemy inside the square —his hatreds, his doubts, his fears— and against another besieging his strength, the writer must fight not so much for his identity but, first, for the search of the elements that constitute it. The hero of Latin–American literature is the artist himself. Arturo Cova's decision to leave the cabinet work of the city to go to *The Vortex* would not have much emotional intensity nor such metaphorical charge if the protagonist was not a poet.

With the advent of political pacification and the slow integration of our republics, professionalization of writing emerges. In Mexico, the facilitating regime for this language cult will be known by the first name of its leader. It will be called Porfiriato and its representative writer, Manuel Gutiérrez Nájera. As a first magnitude star of Modernism, Duke Job pondered on the role of the writer. As the Gautier of enamels and cameos he decided that his task was to engrave his artistic material, although outside the cannons of brutality deafened in the air. From Gutiérrez Nájera on, the prestige of the writer as a romantic hero is replaced by that of a worker in conflict with the words, as Salvador Díaz Mirón manifested when talking about a triple heroism: the heroism of sentiment, the heroism of thought and the heroism of expression. In the late nineteenth century, the writer questions his work. It is also the time when Sigmund Freud uses the guinea pig closer to him –his own persona– to demonstrate his theories about the unconscious. Hence for the writer, as for the scholar of the mind, the way is as important as the result, what Didier Anzieu calls *the body of the work*.

The generation of the Ateneo de la Juventud endorsed the Remy de Gourmont currency, according to which there are writers who write and those who do not. To explain the paradox, Julio Torri wrote the text "On the Noble Sterility of Ingenuity" where he points out: "If we only belong to the first literary generation of men, when they bloomed in all their irresistible virginity even in the most common and trivial platitudes!" True to this slogan, Torri tried to carve out a perfect work in its form, where brevity and intensity are at the service of the writer and the language. The slogan of Enrique González Martínez, that poetry brings us "to contemplate silence and watch the shadow" becomes one of the themes of the young Contemporáneos, who will explore more deeply this vein of the mining writer who works with the subject closest to him. The voices that articulate the poems of "Endless Death" "Death Nostalgia", "Sinbad the Stranded", "Song to a Mineral God" are adventures of the poet in the sea of language, which is the sea of life. As a brotherhood that defended language making it the heritage of "numberless readers" they conceived the poet's work with the man initiated in a set of mysteries. The extensive poems of the group admit to being read as a dissection of the poet in confrontation with silence. To the extent that writing becomes the subject of the work, the elements that form it are more obsessive. Paradoxically, the discovery of the theme of the writer as a character and the requirement that the artist be more a creator than creative —according to the differentiation of Didier Anzieu— is born at the same time than the concern for autonomy of the aesthetic fact. "Enough lady harp of the beautiful images of furtive illuminated likes" cries Vicente Huidobro, tired of the rhetoric repetitions of formulaic Modernists. In this task of creating the language of a vision of the new reality, the writer uses a mask so that an artist, who can sometimes be another writer, can translate the stages of the creative process. Cortázar gives autonomy to Morelli, a writer who shoots and orders –in both senses of the term– the lived and imagined by the characters in *Hopscotch*; in *The Pursuer* the jazzman Johnny Carter serves to distinguish the critic's universe from the field of the inductive artist. Ernesto Sábato makes a dissection of the writer and his ghosts through the impeccable self-analysis of the painter Juan Pablo Castel, as does Alejo Carpentier in most of his works. Jorge Luis Borges makes his surname subject of his writing and manages for it to exist independently, as demonstrated in the text *Borges and I*.

If writing is a vital task, an exercise where the author's energy is at the service of the creation of life, the writer who falls silent lives in a state similar to death–like state. Moreover, it is a death that cannot be understood, understandably, by someone who does not write. The generation of Octavio Paz takes up and questions the legacy of the Contemporáneos. After the experience of the Spanish Civil War, after an intense participation in the fronts of antifascist intellectuals, Paz lives his first youth. Suddenly, inexplicably, he faces a stone wall where words seem to say nothing. From that confrontation between the poet and the language, between the instinctual energy of adolescence and the maturity learned by the man, the sixteen prose poems titled *Trabajos del Poeta*, written in 1949, are born. They are the *Saison en Enfer* of the poet who has lost the immediate communion of actions and words and before whom the nothingness that questions him remains. Although the subject of writer and writing, as well as the differences and similarities between doing and saying are constant throughout his work, it is in *Trabajos del Poeta* where the topic acquires its highest ontological quality: they are poems of purgation, because Paradise —condemned door— has been closed for the young poet. Thereafter, the highlights will be the result of the accumulated experience. Solace and irony: the writer is a being who keeps his adolescence, due to his obligation to cultivate the haloed instinctive being that his innocence gave birth to. Writing is cultivated innocence, experience illuminated again by youth. If poetry is the union of the innocence with experience, Paz's poems reach that strength and forcefulness because they are not the complaint of one who cannot write but one who, like Rimbaud, sings in torment, finding the words that can get us out of that hole, questioning the usefulness of words, their correlation with beings and things, in order to demonstrate the dichotomy posed by Plato in the *Cratylus*. In the mist of his anguished facing the sterility of meanings, the poet succeeds momentarily destroying the creatures called by his own dealings with them. To jump the fence, the articulation of poetry is enough. The drama starts when everything seems exhausted, lessened, dry as the last oasis in the desert:

I write on the crepuscular table, supporting with force the pen on her chest almost alive, moaning and remembering the native forest. The ink opens its large black wings. The lamp explodes and covers my words with a layer of broken glass. A sharp light fragment cuts my right hand. I continue writing with that stump flowing shadow. Night enters the room, the opposite wall advances its stone snout, large cold air stands between pen and paper. Ah, a simple monosyllable would be enough to blow up the world. But tonight there is no room for a single word.

As in Mallarme, it is not a bourgeois lament of creative impotence, but a powerful call of attention against appearances. Perhaps Efraín Huerta, Paz's generation fellow, thought the same when he warned against the wildlife that call themselves poets without being so:

> For your poets, great city!,
> for them and their irksome
> category of outcasts,
> for their loose virtues of eight sonnets a day,
> for their cries at dusk
> and the endless solitude,

for their hysterical writhing

of sexless Prometheans

or sobbing statues, for their rhythm of

in search of a flute.   [donkeys

Trabajos del Poeta is a fundamental text on the relationship between writer and writing and the duality between the man who lives and the poet who creates because writing becomes the antagonist of the one who practices it. The generation of Los Contemporáneos still believed in the full powers of poetry; the voice that speaks from Paz's poems puts into question the role of the poet as a demiurge and visionary river, to leave him, like all men, facing absorbed the stone wall of a terrifying and incomprehensible reality. Solace and torture of the poet: if all men can forget those crises of conscience to which all are exposed, the poet is condemned to permanent lucidity, to question the relationship between words and things and the role he fulfills to explore these mysteries. The search initiated in *Trabajos del Poeta* continues in the dazzling and visionary prose of *The Monkey Grammarian*, where Paz establishes the relationship between the erotic impulse and verbal momentum as one communion where poetry consummates the marriage between heaven and earth.

By forcing us to the meditation on language and the ontological relationship that poets maintain with it, Paz underscores the liberating, but at the same time limiting function of language. In a text dedicated to Octavio Paz, written three decades later, Salvador Elizondo will try to define the name of the strange creature that draws lines of words to create a parallel reality to that where the act of writing occurs. In a line born with the prose poems in *Trabajos del Poeta* (1949) and reaches *The Empty Book* by Josefina Vicens (1958), Elizondo produces a hall of mirrors where writing is the character in a text that starts and gives the title to his book *The Graphograph*:

> I write. I write that I write. Mentally I see myself writing that I write and I also can see myself seeing myself write. And I see myself remembering that I see myself writing and I remember myself seeing myself remembering that I was writing and that I was writing

that I write that I was writing. I can also imagine myself writing that I had already written that I would imagine myself writing that I had already written that I would imagine myself writing that I see myself writing that I write.

The graphograph is the man who traces signs with an absolute awareness of the consequences of that act that is not innocent at all. The graphograph vindicates the mechanical trade of writing, but when fully aware of this act, immediately transforms it into a creative task. The writer who sees himself writing and sees his possibilities in all possible verbal tenses manages to create the possibility of a new being, causes the birth of metaphor. In defining his character, as the graphograph and dedicating it to Paz, Elizondo implements a phrase from *Trabajos del Poeta*:

Absorbed in a meditation −consisting of a meditation about the futility of meditations, a contemplation in which he who contemplates is contemplated by what he contemplates and both by the Contemplation, until all three are one.

While *The Graphograph* can be read as a brilliant amusement, the profound idea of Elizondo is to manifest the ontological anxiety of a being which is his first and most severe judge. Like the Villaurrutia expressing "the doubt of being or not being reality," the graphograph questions the multiple, infinite combinations of a hall of mirrors facing each other. When Villaurrutia establishes his polysemy "mi voz que madura / mi voz quemadura / mi bosque madura / mi voz quema dura" is not only building verbal puns just like fireworks: he is questioning the relativity of the linguistic sign and the mission of the poet as such that leads him to explore the essences of reflexes. In his physical act, the writer overcomes death, in the same way as the Egyptian scribe who looks towards the horizon before concentrating on his task; or Melville's Bartleby who decides not to do it anymore, once he feels he has completed his mission in the Wall Street office where he is serving his sentence to live and write, to write to live. But if the poet who speaks from the texts of Paz and the graphograph that by finding their generic definition they exist in the world, transcending despair by naming it.

While there are scholars who can live with a well–meaning dilettantism, exercising their role as readers and continuing with the circuit of writing, there are also those who find in writing the only reason for their existence, and in its absence, a form of death. Josefina Vicens provides the most notable example of this struggle against the angel. Although the author of another novel and several screenplays and film adaptations, Josefina Vicens is the author of one book, one of the most intense, hopeful and desolated novels of our literature. Its title is precisely *The Empty Book*. Its protagonist is José García, a man like everyone else, who works in an office, has a wife and children, but is distinguished from his congeners in having the need to write, the physiological need, torturous and permanent, of writing. He does not write for fame or recognition, but to know that he exists on the planet, that his performance in his brief adventure on Earth will have a more noble justification than eating, breathing, making love, procreating other beings in his image and similarity. The years when Josefina Vicens writes *The Empty Book* are the same as those when poet Rubén Bonifaz Nuño writes *Fuego de Pobres*, whose initial poem poses the same existential thirst:

> But not forgetting, but remembering,
>
> but with rain and all, so human
>
> are things outside, so on edge
>
> that I wish some would call me
>
> just to give me the joy
>
> of answering that I'm here
>
> or shout who is there
>
> only to see if they respond.

This is the only real reason why José García writes. The duality manifested in every writer is illustrated here because the character has two notebooks: one where he records what happens to man and one where, in his opinion, thoughts worthy of transcending reality or sublimating it fit. Written in an uncompromising style, the text of Josefina Vicens has defeated the easy poignancy or the sentimental whining of a sterile writer who gets exhausted after the first page. The drama between experience and writing, between the experienced and the transformed acquires characteristics of verisimilitude because the character does not think of the fame he can get with his writing but before, and he is very determined, by the need to break the siege where he is like the others. With Baudelaire, José García asks the God of Creation and the Devil of Poetry for the strength and courage to write words that make him superior to those he despises, for which he despises all mankind.

If the tragic figure of José García approaches the Promethean myth of the man whose entrails get routinely devoured by the thirst to create, the writing of Augusto Monterroso is born driven by a no less ruthless demon: that of irony. In an interview with Jorge Ruffinelli, Augusto Monterroso refers to the story "Leopoldo (His Work)" in *Complete Works and Other Stories*: "I wrote it... around 1948, at a time when I myself felt that I was unable to write and I could not decide to be a writer." Leopoldo Ralón is a 34 year old who wants to be a writer, but his vocation is not authentic from the moment he is sure of his genius. Involuntarily, despite himself, his struggles for the perfectionism of writing reveal Monterroso's own struggles with the word: his frustrations with writing create, in spite of himself, a school for the writer. Creating a character who wants to create is a painful metaphor of creative impotence, but also a way to survive, to justify life.

Leopoldo Ralón knows what he wants to write and knows what it takes to do it, but he is not a writer: he can live without writing. With this bitter irony, Monterroso emphasizes the heroism of this hero of modernity, certain that it is not possible to add one more syllable to the ocean of language and knowing it, he begins his adventure. We smile as we see the misadventures of Leopoldo Ralón because under it is the great bitterness about the impossibility of writing, and such helplessness leads to death. True humorists are the greatest pessimists and only a pessimist has the ability to make us laugh. With his tragicomic characters, Monterroso states, without theoretical precepts or a priori definitions that the aesthetical duty of the writer lies in an absolutely ethical congruence. If the writer is the one who can best express the essence of life, it is also he who has a greater capacity to glimpse the destruction, the ending. If Bartleby can be read as a definition of ethical and aesthetic principles of Herman Melville, several moments of Monterroso's writing are dedicated to track the personality of those others who, for various reasons, become more than heteronomous or alter egos, in creatures with sufficient autonomy and humanity as to be contemplated with the same accuracy and objectivity as a scientist would. The most eloquent example in this sense is that which constitutes what Monterroso calls a novel in the subtitle and titles with a verse of William Shakespeare: "The Rest is Silence", Torres' omnia opera, opera that is also a book of homage where Torres's friends and relatives participate. Torres is not Monterroso, even though the letters of the surname of the first one fit in the name of his father. Torres has a voice and style so unique that Monterroso and the voices he calls to make Torres' collective portrait, appear as an autonomy. A reader familiar with Monterroso's writing will find familiar expressions. In fact, Torres does not write like Monterroso, but thinks like only Monterroso could. The writer's commandments – which Torres does not follow in practice– constitute Monterroso's own ideology, that of the writer he would like to be, the writer he is in spite of himself and yet, they are his ghosts.

The complete works of Monterroso, from *The Black Sheep and Other Fables* to *Perpetual Movement* and *The Letter E* is dedicated to establish the anatomy of the possible writer. In other words, the newspaper, the short essay, the marginal confession, the notation on a train ticket, become fragments of a latent discourse, "the essay of the tale of the poem of life." In the works of Monterroso there is no intention to say the last word and although texts like the fables of *The Black Sheep* are counted among some of the most perfect in the language they also have the sense of an open work that all generative texts have. The fable of the fox author of two books, which attentive readers have recognized as a tribute to the reluctance of Juan Rulfo and the writing of his two master works, is a parable of the writer in general. This writing is incessantly different in the book by Barbara Jacobs, *Life with My Friend* (1994). If *The Rest is Silence* is not an autobiography of Monterroso, nor the defense of an alter ego, *Life with My Friend* is not a book about the person of Augusto Monterroso but about the writer that the author shares her life with. With his absent presence, gathered by the memory of the writer, the profiles of Augusto the man are erased and the defined features of Monterroso the writer, his phobias and hobbies, his likes and dislikes, appear. *Life with My Friend* is a metaphor of the writer's life, with the writer: while nothing happens in the physics of actions, everything happens in the metaphysics of consequences. The writer appears as a being unable to cope with the practical challenges of everyday life –hanging a painting, calculating his distances, hammering a nail that has to be held– but ready to face the almost impossible feat to travel without leaving your space, to create more livable worlds than this one. The writer is the being of the most sensitive antennae, but also the closest to translate misery. Between Burton from *Anatomy of Melancholy* and the Seneca from *Letters to Lucilius*, is the secret that writing is an aesthetic duty that allows ethics to become a pleasure rather than an obligation. Literature is not, like love, a remedy for melancholy. Such condition makes more heroic the conclusion reached by Bárbara Jacobs in *Life with My Friend*: there is no light without immersion in darkness, and the true optimist, the only one in which it is possible to believe, is the one who draws his illuminations of the blackness of his pessimism.

Walter Muschg's *The Tragic History of Literature* includes the soul afflictions of the writer and seems to give us as a final lesson that his devotees are a gallery of freaks who must remain behind bars or in that other prison of the circus. Instead, Barbara Jacobs concludes that the writer is the happiest person in the world because he is precisely the one who has explored harder the heart of darkness, who has battled against the angel and can testify to the combat:

Let go of your sufferings, which are often vain, sterile; of nonsense; of evil; find the bright side of things, the bright side of situations;

welcome joy as an attitude in life, happiness as an exercise, it is not easy.

One of the biggest artistic achievements of the XIX century is the autonomy of artistic language. The work stripped of the anecdotal charge that gave rise to it. Why, then, the concern of making the writer a part of the work as a person and a character? In the collective imagination of our end of the century new heroes are not born. Hence it becomes necessary to revive those who had already demonstrated their infallibility to raise the spirit of the community that gave birth to them. The writer is one of these heroes. It is not enough to read the work of our writers but to integrate their Work–Life. One alternative way to read our writers is to read in our writers. Interrogating the body of their work; speculating on the paths that could lead to their creation; if existence is part of their work, the end result is the Work–Life, the inseparable binomial between existence and creation, between the man who suffers and the writer who creates.

This that seems to be an unquestionable truth has to be emphasized in a mercantilist society like ours that opens Schools for Writers, lures and captures new fans for a guild of a specialized literature in a dangerous mutation of subreaders; today, marketing is more interested in selling novels that in the permanence of language in its highest manifestation. As a possible antidote —no efficiency is guaranteed— let's formulate the following draft. Let's assume that someone found it on the last page of José García's notebook, on the bench of a station called Anagnorisis, on the way to the land called Utopia that Monterroso calls San Blas, and Bárbara Jacobs designates as the continuation of the *Sentimental Journey*— there is none other— of Laurence Sterne or the one undertaken by Xavier de Meistre around his bedroom.

1. There are no good or bad writers. There are writers and those that are not do not exist. The ignored geniuses constitute a strange bunch that mediocrity and the thirst for immediate success have created to justify their precarious existence.

2. Do not believe those who say that writing is a pleasure. These claims are as false as those

of the writer trying to justify his laziness by saying he has no time to write. To make her task less unpleasant, Madame de Sévigné would play with the beads of an amber necklace, until she could come up with the right word. López Velarde, less sumptuous but equally selective in his preferences, walked the streets of the city at night looking for the right word where he could settle and find permanence in the fleeting emotion.

3. A Frankenstein's creature made up of various parts of different times and spaces, writing is a monster for whose autonomy the creator is solely responsible.

4. As a professional reader, the great critic is a rejected lover, not because of his ineptitude for the amatory arts, but because he knows the logistics, lures, strategy, arsenal and the consequences of confrontation with the *Thankless One*. When he writes about the others, the critic –a writer in his own way– is like the lover who is conscious that a caress,

an unlikely intercourse, have nothing to do with what he shared with the Prostitute.

5. It is important to write with open eyes, but aware that there is in front of them a blindfold that makes the invisible visible.

6. Literature is the only battlefield where winning is losing and losing is wining. Choosing the way is difficult, but it is more difficult to stay on track with burning patience, to endure its passiveness or maintain the strength and skill needed to continue on track.

7. "The rest is literature;" "The rest is silence." Verlaine and Shakespeare left the ship adrift, but they open the door and invite others to the well. There are no formulas, Dr. Jekyll. Perhaps, experiments where the secret is in the heart and the ways to fight it, to palpitate without knowing it is not ours, but the heart of the world.

8. The exploits of a writer do not occupy the first page of newspapers. The day of the centenary of the death of Rimbaud, November

10, 1991, this event was overshadowed by the news of the death of Yves Montand. And to add to it, attention was also called to the public confession of Earvin Magic Johnson, who declared that he was HIV positive. There is a secret diary of the writing animal. The text comes to the one who needs it.

9. Although Alberto Moravia wrote in *La Noia* a metaphor of the painter who could not paint the subject of this emptiness populated by furies and sorrows is repeated among writers. A possible explanation is that among the arts, writing is the only one that uses the medium we use for everyday communication. We do not greet with musical notes nor use lines and colors for the office instructions. Luis Cernuda noticed how the words with which we say, "Good morning, Don Francisco, how is the family doing?" are the same used to write: "It is the pain of love that cannot be cured but only with the presence and the figure."

10. Reading is another way of writing. It is to write again. Not to repeat the author's intention, but to find ways for the text that perhaps not even the writer conceived.

11. Firmly believe in the tenth commandment of St. Horacio Quiroga: "Do not think of friends when writing, nor on the impression your story will make." Although not your main goal, write with the consolation that those who will truly translate your words, share your suffering and joys.

12. Do not write to comfort, instruct or modify. If you are faithful to this requirement, you will comfort, instruct and modify. Write for no one. Only that way you will be writing for someone.

V

When Father died a group of guardian angels stayed on this side to protect me, to test me, to force me to grow with new blows. Diego Valadés and his Patricia, my dad's favorite student, made it possible for the sordidness that surrounds death to be transformed into a wall to defend the fallen and to preserve his memory with integrity. I also owe Diego my first encounter with my father's substitute and tutelary figure of my existence. One morning, I arrived at the office of Rubén Bonifaz Nuño, the great poet who I admired and read since my teens. When I had the privilege of exchanging my first words with him, I knew what the sensible wisdom was, the return trip. However, I was surprised to also find a cheerful and friendly human being, irreverent and respectful. I was astonished to see him surrounded by very personal toys, from a Florentine dagger for the left hand to a Charlie Brown piggy bank and an enviable collection of kaleidoscopes. By circumstances of magical chance and the generosity of my friends, I started working in the Philological Research Institute founded by the poet. Although I realized immediately that Rubén Bonifaz Nuño occupied my father's emotional place, he never strived to exercise it. He became, instead, a big, protective and discreet, friendly and rigorous brother. Above all, he taught me to laugh at myself, even in the worst circumstances. During a failure in my love life, Rubén called me every evening to check on me, he advised me, he laughed, and we laughed together. When I emerged from my personal disaster, I appreciated his constant calls. He responded that he had spent time in similar hells. Later I was incorporated into the brotherhood that, spontaneous and select, was formed around Rubén Bonifaz Nuño. A trip to New York, which was attended by most of those brothers –Bernardo Ruiz, Marco Antonio Campos, Sandro Cohen, Carlos Montemayor, René Avilés Fabila– convinced Rubén of who were the elected captains of his spiritual guerrilla. Religiously, over five years, we met every Thursday at eight p.m. in Miguel Ángel Quevedo's La Lechuza. Little by little the code that came to acquire the name of Cofradía de los Calaca was polished. Not Las Calacas nor Los Calacas but Los Calaca.

Another igneous angel sent by Dad was Alejandro Cadaval, who made things easy for me in my work, when he was general manager of sports and recreational activities in our University. To this solidarity, Manuel Andrade, my father's student, contributed. He was an integral artist and to whom we owe the shield design of our university puma. Among many other things, Alejandro taught me that pain is never enough. That it is always possible to endure more. Such principle, so simple and so difficult, has sustained me through the years, in small and large tasks. The main lesson took place on a bright morning in Zacatecas, whose sharp and high blue made more real than ever the verse of Ramón López Velarde, "a cruel sky and a red soil." We had gone jogging as a group, among others, writers Guillermo Samperio and Severino Salazar. We were headed by Alejandro, the best athlete among us: handsome, happy, and cynical. In his youth, he was an Olympic long jump champion. Frugal in his habits, eager in his race for life. "With enthusiasm, without forcing it, giving every muscle its place," he would tell us. We bypassed the city and arrived at the top of the Bufa hill. The heart going off of the chest was the best homage to the poet just as was the train that suddenly appeared at the bottom of the landscape, "like a gift from a toyshop." We were halfway in the path. Most of us, exhausted and eager to transform ourselves into a large glass of juice, into a bath, those everyday forms of resurrection. I dared to suggest to Alejandro that we could not continue. "You can" he said. I asked him how he could know. "As soon as we arrived, you made a half turn with such a leg movement and a jump that your teammates could not do because they did not want to do it. It is always possible to do more." Similar words can be found everywhere, from self–improvement manuals to "The Art of War." Living them, transforming them into action is another thing. We made our way back and in the end there were no sweeter oranges than those of a passing man "with the best of ingredients: thirst," said Alejandro. And so it is in everything. When he was told that the Everest was wonderful, it was not enough for him to contemplate it in a picture: he would join, however he could, the next Mexican expedition that would leave to the Himalayas. One day he would buy a motorcycle as luxurious as a Rolls Royce. The next day he had sold it and would use the metro and buses when he was not taken by his powerful legs. One morning, probably the brightest and full of refreshing hope, he hit the front of a trailer. He always wanted to be one who would die young. The insurance company, which is the first enemy of the insured, refused to pay the amount stipulated by accidental death. Its zealous detectives and expert witnesses concluded that Alejandro's death was a suicide.

A top high performance athlete touched by the shadow is as dangerous as a cornered wildcat. Once he was one with the gods, he tasted glory, he was a god donning tennis shoes and conquering the world. With just those two weapons, those wings, inseparable from his legs, synchronicity, breathing, resistance. If we change the word *athlete* for *writer*, the analogy is equally possible. Robert Frost said it: "I think of the poet as a man of prowess, just like an athlete." A runner under the empire of melancholy has stitched on the t–shirt and the flesh a teaching of Alan Sillitoe: no race is the same. The same every day route holds a new experience. The writer, like the runner, practices his work in the most gratuitous and disinterested way, because no one forces him. And while I started running in the company of my older brother when my father was still alive, it was after his departure when the long distance race became not only a physical task, but my true spiritual exercises.

Ascetic, spartan and heroic because it was simple and solitary, the race took me to see the city differently. Like Spider–Man in his nocturnal excursions, I understood that to walk the city is different from walking on it, walking by it. The absence of preposition was like the absence of a protective net to mitigate the fall. Running in the city is to live it differently, it is to possess it as if its body had not belonged to anyone before. The advantage of running above other disciplines is that one confronts himself and makes loneliness his strength. Running modifies the body, but also the perception of reality. It changes our anatomy and it changes the way the world receives us, how we interpret it. Running has been my way of being alone, as Pessoa said of poetry. To be alone and not. It is to be fully with the short–lived animal that is given to us in the longest adventure in the planet. To meet it and confront it. To appreciate its strength and to complain about its weaknesses. To exalt it and to make it support the next minute. To reward it. To deserve the breakfast taken under the sun and to feel that we disperse the shadows and really commune with the world. Writing is to advance. Walking and running scare away sterile ghosts and leave us with the indispensable. London felt the long legs of Virginia Woolf exhaust its streets; Prague, the obsessive walks of Franz Kafka. After imagining the structure of thousands of castles in his wanderings, he could incorporate only one humble partition into the building that represented his true working routine. In principle, the trickle is better since it passes through the many veins of the muddy waters. However, the most intense illuminations are not subject to time. No text has given me the fullness of crossing the island of Cozumel and so live that which I have not written. That intensity makes real what is written and what is to be written.

Running through a city is to make love to it in a different way. Many cities revealed their secrets to me in that way: Atlanta and its streets populated by strong and smiling African—Americans that by applauding me on my way forced me to redouble efforts; the late—afternoon races in Jerusalem, when that waning sun that the Nazarene looked at a long time ago caressed me. The route from downtown Providence to Swann Cemetery where a guard told me at the exit, with stentorian voice, "this is no place for jogging;" the ten kilometers of the thick and splendorous Stanley Park, which almost has the same look since the time the eyes of Captain Vancouver discovered it. The crossing of the island, the three dogs who came out to meet me along with the bang and joy of the open sea at dawn; the running along the dry riverbed of the Turia River in Valencia, to reach it, it is first necessary, from the old heart of the city, to cross a treatise on architecture of all ages and a succession of female names putting the body and soul to burn: Plaza de la Reina, Plaza de la Virgen, Basílica de Nuestra Señora de los Desamparados, and the sun smiling since the early hours while making the dome of Pius V seem twice as blue. And New York, the city that has given itself to a cup of coffee purchased at a cheap place and that you drink across the luxurious structure of the Plaza Hotel; the race at dawn in Central Park, when I got lost in it and there was the lucky need to prolong the farewell; the crossing of Brooklyn Bridge that morning when it seemed newly built or as if it had been raised to fill the seven senses that I had.

***

As the sun rises, orange and full like a painting by Gustav Friedrich, a gazelle runs in the opposite direction to mine. Her youth, her elasticity and beauty are even greater compared to my age and my fat. Each day, she is increasingly away from my youth, but then I would not have enjoyed her, valued her, sung her quietly as now. Nor as I enjoy you, little doe, when you're the most runaway prey and you make me the best hunter in the county.

***

A gush of cold air encourages absent presences, incites the senses. August 2011 in Mexico City. February 1984 against the Dallas sky. Coming to a city almost always governed by the sun to see snow, to see it first as a huge sheet covering the world. From the air, the snow extends beyond what the minimum window of the plane is capable of framing. In the airport I am welcomed by a huge, irreverent, uncontainable as a hurricane from his native Cuba, Nelson de Vega. The man who was once a phone name in a few days will be revealed as the host and natural protector, responsible for the visiting professor that I will be in Austin College. Sooner rather than later, with the speed that the love without wings of authentic fraternity gives, he will become a big brother and advisor, unwavering accomplice. A new father that I adopt, and he adopts me forever. Everything in him becomes sometimes natural and gentle, others expandable and hyperbolic. The life that I have lived is a before and after Nelson de Vega.

In that moment, and we will have to make a mutual confession under the clarity of white tequila, I became disillusioned that the person who received me was a university professor in the United States. He, that the National Autonomous University of Mexico sent a man so shy and demure as a professor to face the Texan avatars. In his resounding and uncompromising Spanish, the Cuban said, "They sent us a timid one." The oil and water were able to combine and over the days and weeks the liking became friendship; the friendship complicity; and the complicity so far unbroken fraternity. I did not know you could be so happy next to a father. I did not know that a father could be so much fun. If I count the times I have laughed until I am blue in the face, Nelson has been the cause of most of them. Only he, with my godfather Alí Chumacero, is able to tell a story already known over and over as if it was the first time it was told in our joy and still caused a surprise.

A heart as big as his could not be alone and I found it committed to Lea Anne, tall and cheerful, a lover of Germany and dolls. With everything, the couple was undergoing a time of crisis and I was with him in those moments where pain armors in pride. José Martí's phrase that back then he obsessively repeated "our wine is sour, but it is our wine," always accompanies and strengthens me, like the warm, thunderous and united De Vega family.

With Nelson I have lived great joys just as gloomy visits to the heart. The death of his son David was for me as painful as only my father's had been. A bridge came again to remind us of our fragility: in the middle of a Texas night, David did not see it, but the bridge did see him, particularly the car that at that moment was his second skin. He left this life when his fierce adolescence was giving way to an increasingly more serene and confident young man. When he began to reconcile with his body, to write poems and to think about this adventure that is ours. A few years later my brother Ignacio died.

Nelson did not think twice and he traveled to Mexico specially to pray at his grave. Together we also share the violent passing of Benjamin Burguess in Campeche and the no less unexpected one of George Wingerter, our common soul brother.

On August 24, 2011, Nelson reached the eightieth year. I find it impossible to conceive of someone of that age with his fortitude and his invincible sense of humor. So childish and irresponsible. So playful and careful with everything that is truly worth it, from the fruit, the food and a bottle of Champagne in his apartment's refrigerator that he offers to his friends as the best suite of Houston to the care that he has with his nephew Raphie, bright *child of a lesser god.*

Today his memory arrives unexpectedly because it smells like deep pine and the air can be chewed because it is ice. The aroma is also that of a different house to ours. Under its shelter, the skin is invaded by an unprecedented temperature that has prevented me from sleeping. Outside it has not stopped snowing. I'm at the Thompson House and tomorrow is the first day of classes at Austin College.

February 1984. An unprecedented adventure that I would like to share with Dad has started. To tell him that at 29 years of age I am a visiting professor at a university in Texas, on lands that were ours, as he used to tell me when he spoke in detail of Mexicans that in 1846, after touring the whole country, fatigued and hungry, were about to go into battle against the invading army in a place called La Angostura in Coahuila. I feel his hand on my shoulder in the same soft and firm way as he would take me to enroll at the university. I do not know it yet, but I'm about to have a new father that will push me to the arena with the sullen tenderness of a fiery one. To never give in, but to break before. To live "without a country, but without a master."

VI

—Who died first?

—The first one I do not know, but the last one was the captain.

Priscila Witt Córdova, oral statement on the   sinking
of the Titanic, Kindergarten Kuruwi, April 26, 2012

The table where I now work has always been with us. By agreement of my brothers, when we closed our parents' house, I brought the furniture with me to find a place for it in the house where I live with the woman to whom I belong. It was not entirely easy to place it so as not to change the impeccable patrician atmosphere. Debbie and Juan Hermann took care of moving everything. The piece of furniture was finally placed overlooking a garden where visible and invisible creatures fulfill their desires.

At some point in our childhood my brothers and I desecrated, —or consecrated— the table to play ping–pong. Patricia Galeana remembers that my father sat his students around it to exercise his relentless interrogations, his Socratic dialogues. Then it was the center of the dining room that would bring us together, an unbearable or saving slate of all Pípilas. After the immediate trauma of the first 1985 earthquake, I told my mother and my sisters to hide under it. I did not know that furniture is the main grave of those who die in earthquakes. My conviction was born of the power and resistance which I gave and give to this mahogany table.

On it my father lived the best period of his creative activity. I dare say it was between 1961 and 1971, in other words, the years of my happy unawareness. In a decade he could do his great set of work as Gustave Flaubert and Justo Sierra taught from their respective disciplines. In love with books as typographical objects and a devotee of their contents, among everything I owe him is the love for those creatures who have –like Lord Byron's dogs– all the virtues of their authors and none of their flaws. If I learned to love books from someone it was from my father's devotion and perseverance. They were the first with which I had contact, either in solitary reading or when he asked me to help him clean them and accommodate them; or some Sunday mornings, when I wanted to go down to the patio and waste time as any child who respects himself, and he would call me to review the French lesson of the week. I, who have never had an ability for languages, I also owe my father having learned from childhood a couple of foreign languages. Also the discovery of History, born initially as an obligation. In 1965, in the eleventh year of my life the first edition of his book Una *Visión Panorámica de la Historia de México* was published. Spider – Man was three years old, and by then he was confronting a gallery of villains as infamous as respectable. The Green Goblin had appeared, complicating the already complicated life of Peter Parker and confronting him with the drama of a double personality.

During the Christmas holidays that year, my father assigned me the daily task of summarizing a chapter of his book. The obligation became the seed for the stories that I invented from what my father had patiently researched and fixed. My epic vision of life, my fervor for heroes and national symbols come from that first experience reading and writing, where unbeknownst to me, my father introduced me in the rudiments of how to develop a synthesis or how to start a thematic fact sheet. Saying much with little was a non–written advice. If Le Corbusier said that architecture is the synthesis of the major arts, my father taught me that history is the most comprehensive writing that exists, because it brings together the imaginative capacity of the novelist, the objectivity of the man of science, the prophetic and metaphorical vehemence of the poet, as evidenced by Jules Michelet, Edmundo O'Gorman or Fernando del Paso.

Una Visión Panorámica de la Historia de México would not have been born without the gymnastics that my father exercised in the newspaper Excelsior. Punctually every week, he would send an article on critical history that would be published in the Diorama cultural supplement. In now unimaginable times, before fax and email, my brothers and I were responsible for carrying my father's neatly typed articles. The JJ Jameson of Excelsior was called Hero Rodríguez Toro, director of the supplement. We enjoyed entering the newspaper's old building on Paseo de la Reforma Avenue, making us part of its aged bronzes and marbles, get to don Hero's office, seeing him with his feet on the desk and the television always on. As children, we thought naively that he never worked because, unlike Jameson, was always in a good mood. At the end, with the money my father gave us for the bus, we would go to the used bookstores on Hidalgo Avenue to search for old comics of *The Amazing Spider–Man*.

Beyond my filial fervor, *Visión Panorámica de la Historia de México* is a book that amazes me because of its synthetic power, its clarity of judgment, the way in which characters and situations of our history are intertwined. My father conjured historians of all tendencies, putting on the scale the arguments of some and others and formulated his interpretation and analysis in a historiographical discourse where the events shine with the purity and hardness of a diamond.

That individual fulfillment was not translated for his tribe. On weekends, he literally threw us out of the house and locked himself up to write. I can imagine us in this image in the Chapultepec forest or in balmy trips to my maternal grandmother's house who prolonged the natural and spontaneous joy of mom. Surely those outings had been preceded by one of the multiple, uncontrollable rages that my father used to have before our consequential terror. It would be enough for the phone to ring and for Dad to answer it for Mr. Hyde to transform himself into the polite and gentle Dr. Jekyll that seduced everyone. Over time, I began to justify that brutal person transforming him in an artistic character of a tragedy. As a child I sensed it, even though I did not have the words to understand it, that creators are great egotists who fail to mature in nuclear areas of their life. If they were not so, they could not form around themselves this fortress of solitude that they populate. There are counted and admirable creators who can break the curse— Johann Sebastian Bach and his countless children; Rafael Cadenas, who does the grocery shopping for the immediate ceremony of life rather than worry about the immortality of his poetry —but most choose not to accept the responsibilities, pettiness and meanness of ordinary mortals. Paradoxically, this makes them smaller and meaner. When my father was carried away by the anger, it was because he felt a diminished inability to face —let alone to defeat— the invincible with dignity and poise. Our common phrase, mumbled as exorcism, was "he is angry." He was not angry with us or because of us. He was angry at himself, and we could do nothing to alleviate that pain. That impotence. That terrible mirror is one of the attitudes that I hate the most about myself and the one to which I succumb constantly. I have tried to learn, however, the lesson of one of my father's cousins, Uncle Leandro from Guadalajara. At his insistence on prolonging the after–dinner conversation, my father argued that he had a thousand things to read and write. My brothers and I stayed with our uncle to talk about inconsequential therefore transcendental nonsense. Dedicated to the hauling of construction materials, a worker came to tell him that one of his trucks had a terrible accident, it turned over and had lost everything it was carrying. My Uncle Leandro, composed and without raising his voice, said, "it is fine" and slowly turned to get busy rather than worry. From my father I inherited, although I continuously fight it, his atrocious pessimism. However, I find in that defect a virtue, which is familiar, born of those who have survived a catastrophe: we face major tragedies with integrity and effectiveness. We are concerned and make a scandal, as Rosario Castellanos says, if we burn the rice or we lose the property tax bill.

The barrier that Dad placed since my childhood prevented me from approaching him lovingly, spontaneously, in adulthood. He told the child that I once was: "When someone asks if I'm your dad, tell him I'm your father." In that sober harshness there is something regressive from Jalisco. Years later it reconciled me to identify that custom in the children of José Luis Martínez when they addressed him with a warm but respectful "Listen, Sir" or when seeing how José Rogelio Álvarez's children and grandchildren approached him. I never dared to kiss Dad either and he never gave me a kiss. The only time I could have done it he was lying in his coffin, and between my mouth and face there was the barrier of a glass which closed all possible contact. So, I could never call him Dad, as surely all my friends called theirs. I could never hug him like I did and I still do those who are not my blood, in their time of need. However, Dad said I love you in other ways: putting a peach with red feminine skin in front of me so it would be the first thing I would see when I woke up; picking me up from the bus station after returning from a perilous trip to South America, only bearable when you have the invincible poverty of twenty years of age; buying for me the Harvard Classics from a used bookshop, still smelling of new and with gilded edges: I enjoy them with the same intensity as the toys he gave me when I finished first grade. Or the copy of Azorín's "El Artista y el Estilo", which he signed for me with his energetic and confident handwriting, but with words that even to a stranger would have sounded harsh and distant.

One of the last days of his life I saw him in the distance in a cafe near Insurgentes Avenue, where he used to go in the company of his students and where he would compensate his long overstaying with splendid tips. From the street I saw him alone, leaning on a table in a desolate stillness. His face was no longer in this world and an ash gaze urgently pleaded the mercy of death. I kept going with the immediate jaw of remorse entrenched in the flesh of the soul. My vital instinct moved me away from the one sinking in the ship, but who inside his personal tsunami was preparing everything so the rest of the crew would not get lost. His physical attitude – a reflection of his soul– was that of Durero's angel: surrounded by all the instruments to plot and build what his skills required of him, those for which he was prepared, his bitter gesture turned him into his worst enemy, making him an impeccable target of his unsuspected and intimate pains. Someone very wise and long–lived, Johann Wolfgang von Goethe, wrote that fresh and renewed activity was the only way to survive adversity. Of those last weeks when my father was in the world, I remember how joyful and relieved I saw him one morning, just bathed and bright, standing by his high desk, which evoked Hemingway's: a momentary and consoling certainty that he was capable of overcoming the storms that threatened him and those on his ship.

To say that you cannot write can be an elegant coquetry, a supreme justification for laziness or impotence. One of the books most underlined by my father is a selection of Gustave Flaubert's letters prepared by René Dumesnil. I constantly go to it to speak, in some way, with my father and to see how a giant of Flaubert's quality could exclaim, at the height of a frank despondency, that in a week he had written only two pages of *Madame Bovary*. However, that same being —but not the same person— was capable of writing to his muse, Louise Colet, that letter from October 14, 1846, where I see a picture of my father in the best moments of his writing and his style:

> Work, meditate, especially meditate, condense your thinking, you know that the beautiful fragments are nothing. Unity, unity, everything is in it! All the pieces, which is what is currently missing in all of them, both great and insignificant. Thousand beautiful

places, no work. Stay within your style, make
a soft weave as silk and strong as armor.

My father suffered like no one else the flauberian
torture and delight, amplified by the amphetamines
that Jean–Paul Sartre consumed his whole life
without them being obstacles to his pen and his
genius, they made my father conceive impossible
projects and left him at the end with the humiliation
of defeat. One of the last books he read and
underlined, true to his custom, was the
correspondence of his admired Van Gogh in one of
the lavish French editions he loved. When I could see
with my Patricia in Vienna, in a retrospective
exhibition, the last originals of the great Vincent, it
is surprising how he could achieve that objective
intensity in the middle of the collapse. The final
sinking of my father –and in Van Gogh's letters he
underlines several times the word collapse– began
when he lost the structure and method that allowed
him to keep his beast domesticated. One of those
details, apparently insignificant but revealing for
those of us who knew him, was that he stopped using
his fountain pen and the violet Scrip ink, none other,

that gave identity to his beautiful handwriting. Objects do not secure life. Tools that help us make our adventure more habitable, when they choose us they transform us and transform themselves in subjects. Dad was not attached to objects, but he loved the well–built ones, those where human talent and care concentrated to turn them into eternal joys, as John Keats wanted.

We madmen embrace punctuality and rituals, waiting for the minute that once completed saves us from the tyranny of time or an element that reveals what had passed unnoticed. The route between Aralia Street, the Tlacopac Church and the Insurgentes Avenue tries to be a different battle every day, an alternate way of existing. Today the sun sets on the same façade, but it will never be the same as yesterday's. The one that said no yesterday will say yes today. The owner of the tobacco store, as in the poem by Pessoa, by raising his hand and saying hello, ignorant of the little dramas that take our time, will erase *enormous minutiae* and justify the hours to be filled later. There are some mornings when the day seems to start with the same

115

oppression that invades us. Others, however, the small miracles are enough to continue: the young street sweeper who fulfills his duty with almost a mystical discipline; the dog that after a long abstinence has a banquet with the bag of food that the restaurant has carelessly left; the policeman who says "good morning" with a smile brighter than his offended plate. Rituals needed to survive in the streets that integrate the familiarity of the neighborhood. For those who in their flesh and in their tribal soul have been violated by the Grim Reaper it is not possible to stop watching those shadow creatures that without notice, invade the fullness that with effort we build. They get in, detonate, flood with their greasy ink all the open space. They transform greatness into an insignificant work. They transform the sublime into ridiculous. Into a monster the angel that yesterday we contemplated in the mirror. Or at least a glimpse of that tolerable being that we form together to face our daily life. "There are black zones of shadow close to our daily paths, and now and then some evil soul breaks a passage through" wrote Master Lovecraft, who knew so much about ghosts. If that were not the case, how can Robert Schumann's fate be explained? On February 10, 1854, his wife Clara wrote:

> At night, not long after we went to bed, Robert got up and wrote a tune that he said, the angels had sung for him. Then he lay down again and talked deliriously all night, looking at the ceiling all the time. When the morning came, the angels had transformed into demons singing a horrible music while telling him he was a sinner and that they were going to drag him to hell. He became hysterical, screaming in agony that they were pounding him like tigers and hyenas, and were holding him with their claws. The two doctors who came were barely able to control him.

***

One afternoon in 1978. On a sticky, crowded bus that never arrives, I go to Tlalpan, to visit Dad to the hospital where we committed him, where he was held against his will, where the dark side of the

Force secluded him. On driver's speakers, the driver who drove as if we were going to the slaughterhouse, you could hear a tropical song that exalts the ardent, unconscious and instant present time of life, while inside me everything is overshadowed. It was inconceivable that the world would continue. The sum of personal duels demonstrates the vanity that what happens to us is the worst and the best in the world. The wrath of the earthquake, its telluric force that devastates everything, collapses, cuts and buries is parallel to cyclists and runners, who, like sweaty lovers, live life like no other; like the teen creature assaulted by the unknown sensation of the first solitary orgasm, the stevedore that finishes his daily work after having started it at the Central de Abastos market when most of the city sleeps.

I compare that disheartened twenty–three year old me with the father of that young man that I am now, this morning that I enter for the first time a brand new Metrobus station: everything is new and even the day and life seem to be. The world is older than before and it is newborn. Much of my early life I lived in this Insurgentes Avenue from the

Colonia Roma neighborhood to Ciudad Universitaria. When poetry started to become a dominant passion and cautionary exercise, the world was revealed through images and words that had previously been unknown to me. Thirty–three years ago, a bus was taking me to the heart of darkness. Today I make the journey in reverse direction toward a delayed and promising light. My father lives in me. I'm his father. His wings are open on my back.

***

The first time Dad entered a psiquiatric hospital, it was because we wanted him to. We felt incapable of enduring —and curing— those continuous and radical mood changes that destroyed him and destroyed everything around him. And so what, an outsider could say, if Professor Quirate wants to be another Aureliano Buendía, if he gives himself the luxury of melting the gold he does not have and burns completely the salary that never comes, my coronel, in the French bookstore? One of his closest students, after discussing it with us, took him to the Rafael Lavista Hospital, in the heart of Tlalpan, a place traditionally occupied by saints and lunatics, in other words, by convents and psychiatric hospitals that used to be called *retirement houses.* The following days were uphill, even more than those that followed the physical death of my father. Being crazy is losing control of the demons that every sensitive person must carry inside himself. Insanity, without covering it up and with all that the word itself means, is a living death for those who live it and those who suffer that of a loved one. It would have helped me to know what I would later read in William Styron, when speaking of the hospital as a place where the beast can be contained, at least momentarily. An arena where other fighters face the transformation of angels into demons that Schumann suffered, a metamorphosis that we, who are out of that hurricane as fascinating as devastating, cannot fully understand.

Dad's soul disease was the first unknown, powerful, tangible ghost we faced. The passing of the years taught us to live with those who were arriving in multitudes. We have come to tell them good morning or just ignore them, like the character in the movie *A Beautiful Mind*, who ultimately accepts their presence: called by him, they can place him on this side. Sweet and courageous Susana, the youngest among us, the greatest among us, familiarly called it "La Depre," as a way of exorcism against that bitch that knows how to give invisible bites: the great Francisco Hernández knows it. However, on top of the medicines that after successive trials managed to balance or at least to warn us about the attacks of the Beast, our best ally was Mom's practical stoicism: her fierce innocence was an effective invisible sword against the shadow.

The hardest part was talking to the doctors. With an innocence that the passing of the years would tinge, then fully convinced I would tell them that my father was not any patient but an artist with a particular sensitivity. He had nothing to do with the schizophrenics, alcoholics, drug addicts who shared the same cage with him. Like Martín Quirarte, the violinist Higinio Ruvalcaba, also from Jalisco, like him with his roots in Yahualica, would

not tolerate half–measures, mediocrity in any sense:
he had to be a real artist, a great drunkard, an
insatiable lover or just not to be. Hence the anguish
of the artist, the drunkard or the lover when he feels
the intensity that sustains and justifies his place in
the world is disappearing. *Enivrez–vous sans cesse*
my father could say with Baudelaire. That
drunkenness was the flawless page where concepts
had found their counterpart in the right words, the
class in which the professor and students entered at
the same time and lived the preludes of the uprising,
the parliamentary combat, the fatigue of anonymous
heroes about to begin the battle.

My father was never going to be cured. To do
so would mean to give up his passion, everything for
which he really existed. With his student Eusebio
Ruvalcaba, son of the angelic and diabolical
musician, while my father was in the hospital we
read Julio Cortázar's *The Pursuer* tirelessly. For us,
don Higinio and don Martín were, as the jazzman of
the story, different from ordinary mortals. For the
world, poor devils unable to cope with their
emotional problems and addictions. They were both

things, and the hospital, as the prison, was responsible for aligning them into one sole category:

> ... more than ever alone against that which he pursues that flees from him the more he pursues it [...] he is not a victim, he is not persecuted as everybody thinks, [...] he pursues instead of being pursued, [...] everything that is happening in life is the chance of the hunter, not the hunted animal. Nobody can know what Johnny is chasing, but it is like that, it is there, in *Amorous*, in marijuana, in his absurd speeches about so many things, in his relapses in the little book by Dylan Thomas, in all the poor devil that Johnny is and that makes him big, transforming him in an absurd being in a hunter without arms and legs, in a hare running after a tiger that sleeps.

Dad left the hospital, but the one who returned home was not the passionate arbitrary being that we feared and admired, but a lifeless creature, domesticated and brutalized by tranquilizers.

Unable to create in the broadest sense of the word. In a page by Erwin Panofsky I would later find a possible answer:

> Melancholy is what can be called the ultrawakefullness; its fixed gaze is a vain attempt of a fruitless search. It is only inactive, not because it feels lazy to work, but because the work has lost meaning; its energy is paralyzed not by sleep, but by thought.

That is why when in that dark room in Los Angeles my brother Ignacio's voice told me on the phone that Dad had died, my first reaction was relief. Even now, over the years, I have no regrets. As in the final scene of the movie *One Flew Over the Cuckoo's Nest*, when Chief Bromden decides to free his friend with the only existing cure after the trepanation that has been practiced on him, transforming him into a useless vegetable without the unconscious grace of vegetables. Dad was losing the best of him, that which gave him structure and made him different. He was named President of the Broke People Bank by the Lagunilla stevedores when he was young and opened the cash register of his diminished saddlery to exercise charity in a virile natural, nakedly Christian way. I recall another one of his unforgettable moments. He was back from a trip to Europe with a red wool coat for my mother. In those recent medieval times of irrational customs' control, officers told him he could not cross that luxury item. My father showed them, in vain, the moderate price–for him a fortune– he had paid for it. Torturers naturally expected a bribe. Dad sat down, patient, to wait for the verdict. The phrase "the one who does not cheat does not advance" was unknown in his code of life. Angry, resigned to not getting their share from him, they returned to check his passport, they asked what his occupation was. "I am a professor," he answered humbly. They continued to exercise their insignificant and omnipotent power. At the end they told him: "Come in, you serve the country." And Dad's eyes filled with tears, at the height of the Stockholm syndrome.

"I want to die" is a phrase we use in a general irresponsible way in front of those who articulate it with full conviction that death ceases all pain. Dad

125

really decided that it was time to die, and there was no power at that time that could invoke it. I say at that time because with the passage of time medicine and treatments have significantly improved, as shown by Dr. Kay Redfield Jamison in her book *Touched with Fire. Manic–Depressive Illness and the Artistic Temperament*. Touched by fire, but protected from its flames. However, I have also tried to learn that suicide is the most respectable of decisions: when embedded, as burning medal, in the heart of the one who is willing to go, there is no hospital, medicine or straitjacket that could prevent the decisive act. Without saying it master Flaubert confirms it when involuntarily he writes a possible epitaph for this common and incurable creature: "It does not matter. Let's die in the snow, let's perish in the white pain of our desire, under the murmur of the torrents of the Spirit and the face turned towards the Sun." Two weeks after the crisis described by his wife Clara, Schumann left home without a coat and he threw himself into the Rhine. He was rescued and hospitalized in Endenich, where he died of voluntary starvation in 1856, without having abandoned once the hospital.

More than once I have said, with a divan's delightful resentment, that I would have liked to have a dad who played ball with me. It is not true: if I could choose a father he would be like the one I had the privilege of knowing: contradictory but passionate, insolent but honest, forgetful and brilliant, distant and close. Always on fire. I would ask one thing: that he would have been a better friend to himself. I have lived more years without a father than with him. However, I never had him so much as now. He was the first to go, but he will be the last to die. Priscila is right in her childish response to the equally smart question of another child: we do not know the name of the first one who died in the wreck of the Titanic. Metaphorically, the captain was the last to die because his obligation was the ship: the dreams of his crew, the joyful ghosts of his sheets, the illusion of leaving, the thirst for arrival.

The table that I work on is a definite phrase, heavy as the table itself. To work is a relative word and therefore filled with meanings. In it I write when I write, which means that in it I carry out the task that killed my father. Second definitive definition, equally unjust. To save myself, I turn to other forms of work, without a doubt impure and prostituted, according to Edmund Wilson's demand for the real writer. On this table, where it appears sometimes the lightning of creation, I practice alternate ways, blessed and redemptive, of writing: I read thesis, I write recommendation letters, I write checks, I have breakfast with haste while I give the last touches to the text where I am pleased to offer someone else's text, after being illuminated by it. When I thoroughly clean this table that is now mine; when I strip it of everything that fills it daily and when I wax it and caress its veins and its forms, besides going back and forth through my childhood, I feel that victory begins.

I write on this table from the early moments of the new day. The usual bird always announces it in the same tune, it is the monarch of the garden. The darkness is gone and in front of us a new opportunity unfolds. Most of the time I do not write, but I achieve the perfect elizondian ideal "I write that I write." And sometimes, thanks to that dedication epiphany emerges. I looked up from the table: in the background the garden offers its repeating life lesson, of incessant work, oblivious to our sterile dramas. While defeat prepares its ambush, half of the road is done. At the beginning of the day, I repeat the prayer that in Vailima the twice and always young Robert Louis Stevenson coined. A prayer that I will surely be unfaithful to, but that I will never stop embracing:

A new day comes back, and brings its small series of irritating chores and obligations. Help us to act as men; help us to meet our task with smiling and friendly faces; let joy prevail at work. Let us on this day go joyful to our matters at hand; take us, fatigued, happy and without dishonor, to rest in our beds, and grant us, at the end of the day, the gift of sleep.

VII

Happy Hour is the short time when two for one is charged: privileged access time because it is the work time, forced, obligatory, and almost always mercenary. It is not a time for drunks, but for the drunk alone. The time to ask questions that were formulated before, back then without finding an answer, before the cold gaze of the psychoanalyst. For this reason, the bar at Sanborns is at certain hours the cheapest and best place to write. Or simply to be there.

Alcohol and Love are two miraculously related words in Spanish. The same number of syllables and accents, identical vowels. The most open and elementary in the alphabet, from an early age christen our closest wants and needs. Love and alcohol amplify or cut the existence, give meaning to the hours, defeat them. For a previously obscure reason, only here I ask for the pair formed by the white Herradura and Bohemia beer. However, while the water that cuts, the foam and liquid gold become part of my body and consume its fullness over the defeats of the week, a certainty illuminates me: the strange occasions when Mom drank, the Bohemia was her invariable choice.

Mom made of life a two for one. While her children and her husband made an effort to combat time, so that it could leave like an uncomfortable guest, she expanded it, giving it meaning, with a wisdom that Baudelaire did not dare to sense. She waited liturgically for the Beatles' Hour. Although she never learned English, she listened to them as if they were Gregorian chants.

During the 1986 school year, while I was a visiting professor at Austin College, she would punctually send by mail the magazine *Proceso* and *La Familia Burrón*. In those prehistoric times prior to the internet, it was her way of keeping me in contact with Mexico, but also with the most profound that we were as a family. The Burróns were part of us, the same as beings and objects in the Lagunilla neighborhood where we were born and grew up: the floors and walls of irregular stone which in old times were lavish constructions –these were the palaces–, the patios were where the world was wide and never foreign, the rooftop terraces as a fifth facade and the closest place to heaven. The magazines came accompanied by a letter with my mom's big, fresh and clear handwriting. Her names was Luz, but my brothers and I started to call her *Gamucita*: her white and stretched hair, her glasses and her figure each day more petite, physically reminded us of Doña Gamucita Botello widow of Pilongano, suffering and devoted mother of the poet Avelino Pilongano, author of, among other titles, *Coven of Neurons* and *The Squared Circle of Amoebas*.

Mom, cried like none of us, the death of my father. She cried for him, but more for her, for what they had lacked, for what she never had from her husband. "The best of marriage is widowhood, even if one is the dead one," preached the great Alí Chumacero. With the death of my father, my mother lived her new youth: in the plenitude of her 60 years, she quickly went up the subway stairs; she went alone to a movie theater to see the movie *The Warriors*, surrounded by urban gangs in the neighboring seats; she promptly deposited the payment of the *Encyclopedia Britannica*, when I convinced her that it was the best investment for the future, before the cybernetic era tried to assault that trench.

An image remains with me of the moment when, without shedding a tear, Mom truly cried for Dad. Not her in him, but the man she loved, despised, forgave and came to love. The man so unlike her, so arbitrary and unfair. So constant. Several years after Dad's death, Mom and I are watching, with no one else at home, the film adaptation of Antonio Tabbuchi's *Pereira Mantains*. Seeing Marcello Mastroianni in the role of the disillusioned and apathetic character in the novel, overweight in body and soul, melancholic and defeated, we discovered his uncanny resemblance to Dad. "Do you have money?" was the invariable question of my father's wife. And she asked that question on March 13, 1980 when she saw him alive for the last time. She would have wanted to tell him to come back, that she was going to iron his coat, as he went to the University with the same wrinkles of the heroic battle suit that Mastroianni wears in the film, under the humiliating and muggy Lisbon heat. Mom wanted to iron his soul, though she knew that inside him only shone a dark and enemy sun, an unconditional ally of the one who was departing. In the final part of the movie I took Mom's hand. Without telling her anything I was saying that the surviving part of us was like the new Pereira that free of kilos and eyeglasses, rejuvenated by the love for the neighbor, was the Martín Quirarte left in us: not the mortal enemy of himself but the generous and altruistic man who gave himself to others.

Doña Luz died unexpectedly at age 85 while listening to Wolfgang Amadeus Mozart. Outwardly in peace, although inside her there were biological disasters that were destroying in a definite manner her prolonged enviable strength. The first of us who was gone in her bed and was fading off peacefully. I have not been able to cry for her because she does not hurt me and I reproach her for that too. She always had the elegance to be unnoticed. To be the last to go to sleep and the first to see the dawn. Facing misfortune with a resolution born of a natural stoicism without adjectives. Still, the pain that will never leave me is having to tell her face to face that her eldest son no longer existed. To see her breaking like that.

***

On May 11, 2011, my brothers, my nephews and I gather at the notary to finalize the sale of the family home in the Colonia Roma neighborhood. That day it was thirteen years since we buried Ignacio, the oldest of my brothers. In the coincidence I read the end of a cycle, the closing of a circuit. I thought that when I finally let go of that house I would experience something like a fullness, but nothing special happened. Apparently. I left the notary's office, free of chains. I walked by Insurgentes Avenue and got to San Ángel, to the doors of La Invencible, with the desire to make part of my body the most ritual and rewarding tequila of my life before returning home. I was overcome by an obsession of getting a traditional Lotería game and the Oca *game* for Priscila and Nicole, the smaller tributaries of my Patricia who would spend the afternoon with us.

I no longer entered La Invencible and walked to the market, that archive which preserves in the present the best of the past, and found the games. To initiate the girls in that elemental and ancient board game was a way to celebrate and prove that life is incessantly recycled, it gives up its darkness to the thrust of what continues, as the planet turns to dawn again.

Our brother Ignacio left us at age 47, on May 9, 1998. He committed suicide at the age of Lovecraft, Pessoa, Musset. Early still to go. Late to start again. From this decision of another member of the tribe, we realized it was impossible to lower our guard; we had to shield ourselves again against the latent enemy, against what William Styron calls "visible darkness" in a book that became a repeated reading.

The yellow dog is born on the street. It is solitary, stoic and strong. There is always someone who holds out a hand to it. That is why the phrase "Luck of a yellow dog" should move more to admiration than pity. The metaphor ideally describes my brother Ignacio. He was born with that destiny and grew up with excessive pressure from Dad. One is the person who procreates a number of children, but each will have a different father, who will live through him in his own way. That is how it happened to us. My father concentrated all his frustrations—love and anger— on his first born and there was never communication —much less communion— between them. Ignacio could have signed, word by word, the letter to a father that Franz Kafka wrote to all those who see their father as a cruel and powerful god that one must end up hating to kill fear itself.

Ignacio. My older brother who knew everything: dinosaurs, the functioning of a racecar, the English lyrics of the new songs, distances between planets, the Tepexpan man in the Chopo's Natural History Museum. When he confessed to have no answer to my question, reluctant to admit his fallibility, I would insist: "And more or less?"

In the only childhood picture where we are together, at his five years of age Ignacio is a vanguard rock and roller: ultra—combed with brilliantine and a sweater that strives to maintain its dignity again. I, two years old, rough, baggy, my hair as rebellious as Silvestre Revueltas drunk and just awakened, in a photograph that Eusebio Ruvalcaba keeps devoutly. Ignacio takes my hand and smiles happily at the camera. I manifest the hostility and bad face of my childhood pictures. On the back, a hand that is not my mother's nor my father's wrote, to give evidence of the fact: "Chentito and Nachito.

" In what moment was the deal broken? When did Mr. Hyde manage to inoculate in my brother's blood that filter incapable of bringing him back to light? When did my brother and I stop tangibly holding hands, the paths diverged and he let himself be overcome by the demon that each of us and in group had to defeat? Horrible defects, rectifiable, he systematically wrote in a notebook, and he tried to solve the ones that tortured him the most.

The doubly extraordinary snowfall that took place between January 10 and 11, 1967 in Mexico City is linked to Ignacio because I never admired him as I did then. My father had sent us to the Library at the Museum of Anthropology to transcribe some microfilms. Ignacio was the knight and I his squire. As the excellent and neat typist that he was, he was typing as I read in an inexpensive and invaluable book, *A Study in Scarlet*. In front of his time machine, my brother would bring to life the works and days of Mexican heroes. Outside, snow—covered Chapultepec was London and we were leaving, pubescent Holmes and Watson from Anahuac,to withstand unprecedented temperatures, small locomotives invading the air with their unrepeatable personal misting. Then we truly touched happiness.

"Little brother," we called each other, when love knew no barriers or conventions, when the word brother had not yet made us enemies nor uncomfortable relatives. We no longer held hands, like in the childhood picture, but when we would start our systematic explorations through the city, his older hand was on my shoulder, mine on Javier's, my younger brother. "Little brother". We walked as if we owned the city, wanting everything, needing nothing. Invincible.

The suicide victim is a precision instrument, his own infallible guillotine. The letter left by Ignacio was in his printer. He did not even take it out from the machine. After his death, before my inevitable feelings of guilt Dr. Miguel Matrajt made the analogy of the suicide victim with the machine: a meat grinder is designed to perform a function, but it will also crush anything you put in it. Nothing would have made my visits, my good intentions, our running through Ciudad Universitaria where the movement was immediate and an effective remedy against the Lady in Black. "If you could have bought him an apartment on Fifth Avenue in New York and deposited one million dollars per month, would you have saved him?" Vanity from the one who continues here. If after Dad's death life became an inevitable substitute, a hyperbolic event which significantly contributed to by the sun of the birth of his Anabel, Ignacio's daughter, our first niece, the departure of my brother turned everything where the existence palpitated into mourning and dispossession. The bright colors of fruit in the market were no more for him and making them part of me was an obligation and not a pleasure.

Three times I saw him dead. The first, when I went with a locksmith to his apartment and realizing that life was no longer with him, instinctively, as in the days of childhood, I touched him on the shoulder. The second, returning with the police. Their inevitable vulgarity became solidarity, eased the crippling pain and me into forced to action: helping to take him down made me understand the importance of the mourners as partakers of that which otherwise would not be a ceremony. There is an expression in English, in principle untranslatable: "Pull yourself together." I repeated it inside me as if it was a prayer. A shield. Now I know that our language has an even stronger equivalence: "Arm yourself." Put in place all the parts of the whole that are being fragmented. Take what you can to face what can tear you apart. Death is offering you from life everything that you had not understood.

The third time I saw his corpse was at the end of that day. Late at night I recognized his body. In the natural squalor of the Medical Forensic Service, that site that seems to underline all the ugliness and misery of Mexico City, looking at his body and moving my head affirmatively I said yes he was my brother, who had been, even in that present time, endless, teaching how to breath with more respect. I understood the words of the wife of Chekov that Raymond Carver transcribes in his story about the writer's death: "There were no human voices nor everyday sounds. There was only beauty, peace, and the grandeur of death. "

The message left by Ignacio says that he feels invaded by the same disease that took Dad. When the prosecutor asked me again and again if my brother was suffering from some illness, I said yes: a deadly, incurable one called sadness. As shipwreck survivors we need the name of the evil of our lineage, to understand the behavior of that larva that grows, implacable and invisible, within us, even if later signifier and meaning lose the ties that unite them. What was possible for me to attest to several times was the tangible, brutal, final way that it hit my brother: we the Quirartes know how to recognize, as animals feel the scent of predators, the instant when the beast of apathy and paralysis comes to settle in our back. I am not fully transcribing my brother's letter. I will keep it and I've read it countless times but, as Marc Etkind writes, suicide notes should not be known to outsiders, unless special circumstances make them public documents. I pick only what can serve those of us who are still on this side: three times my brother says he cannot bear life. Three times he apologizes for what he is about to do. The same desperately lucid reiteration, appears in the letter that Virginia Woolf left to her husband on March 28, 1941 before throwing herself into the river, supplied with stones to help her guarantee her death. Three times she mentions the word happiness or condition of being in it:

> Dearest,
>
> Once again, I feel certain I am going mad. I feel we can't go through another of those terrible times. And I shan't recover this time. I begin to hear voices, and I can't concentrate. So I am doing what seems to be the best thing

to do. You have given me the greatest possible happiness. You have been in every way all that anyone could be. I don't think two people could have been happier till this terrible disease came. I can't fight any longer. I know that I am spoiling your life, that without me you could work. And you will I know. You see I can't even write this properly. I can't read. What I want to say is that I owe all the happiness of my life to you. You have been entirely patient with me and incredibly good. I want to say that —everybody knows it. If anybody could have saved me it would have been you. Everything has gone from me but the certainty of your goodness. I can't go on spoiling your life any longer. I don't think two people could have been happier than we have been.

In New York, after the death of my carnal brother, long conversations with Frédéric Yves Jeannet, brother by choice. United by the fervor to Jean–Arthur Rimbaud and the suicide of our parents, the new wound caused by Ignacio's decision forces us necessarily to reinvent life, as demanded by the master. "I cannot think of killing myself because they have already done that to me before." Frederic says it fully convinced, he who has resisted attacks of the Dark Lady and already exceeded the age of 37 years that his father was when he abandoned this world. We recall the threatened beauty of Mariel Hemingway, her high, unsurpassable cheekbones, her angular face that promises to withstand the ravages of time, and how she has struggled to survive knowing and feeling herself part of a family of suicide victims. To understand the ways of the crouching beast and the means to defeat or prevent its arrival.

The children of suicide victims know an exit route. Our dual job is to explore other trails. In *Hansel and Gretel*, the Grimm Brother's tale, the children lost in the woods return home thanks to the foresight of having pointed the way with stones. The second time they cannot rebuild it because the scattered pieces of bread to mark the return have been eaten by birds. Although it is not the intention, the suicide victim traces a path for his loved ones. Survivors rebuild it, perhaps also unintentionally; at the same time they search and favor the arrival of birds of the spirit to erase the signs of the path leading to the fatal encounter with the mirror: not the one reflecting what we are, or what we think we are, but the one who loses the battle against the sinister half that will destroy us, that Mr. Hyde brutalized by fear and helplessness to a life that has no other choice but to annihilate it.

We are in the 29 floor of a building on 93rd Street. Below us the city unfolds. My father threw himself from a ridiculously low bridge. If he had not obtained the glory and relief of death, a humiliating disability would have awaited him. Life throbs down under and in us. We are two minimum participants in the great representation. We are not essential for the world or first figures, but in this moment we are the first men in the world. The suicide victim discovers he is the last man on Earth but also, when he knows the end of his pain has come, has a moment of fullness that makes him god and creator of himself, powerful and omnipotent. As the writer when he manages to overcome that I do not know what that keeps him alive and what is necessary to kill to give life.

***

We were born in downtown Mexico City, in a house anchored in the eighteenth century, neighboring the old San Lorenzo Convent, a pulque bar called La Antigua Roma and the bar La Esperanza. In a major city that forgets everything, the three bastions subsist, with the same use as they always had for more than half a century. Between Lagunilla and the zone of the better established commerce, we were initiated into the cult of what Efraín Huerta called "the greenest and deepest part of the old city." In the church of San Lorenzo, the martyred hand of Jesus Christ taught me not the joy of Christianity but its terrors: a primal fear of guilt and of the tears of the Virgin who was showing her pain publicly. From the balcony of the house we heard the ESIME (Escuela Superior de Ingeniería Mecánica y Eléctrica) guys, in the only and heroic 1968, shouting the slogan "For San Juan de Letrán, by San Juan de

Letrán." On the same street we saw the evening of October 2 the assault trucks heading towards Tlatelolco. The world fit for some years between few and intense streets.

Our house was a majestically ruined building and now in full process of deterioration. Under the main staircase the remains of a fountain where horses could drink were preserved, rings to hold them and a court wall that crowned the patio, which made a historian friend of my father exclaim that we had a little Parthenon for our personal use. At night, we listened with hypnotic fascination to Don Pancho, the old doorman tell ghost stories in the back of the building, adjacent to the San Lorenzo Temple. To increase our terrors and delights, we were devoted readers of the comics entitled *Tradiciones y Leyendas de la Colonia.* To the rigorous historical research a treatment that emphasized the gruesome and sadistic part of the stories of the old city was added. Once we returned terrified to our house, we refused to stay alone for fear the headless man would appear on the roof of the building, those sentenced to death by the Holy

Inquisition Court in the neighboring Santo Domingo Plaza or the monks who used to walk with their blue flames, on our own building. With the passing of the years, I would again find the child I was in the story *These Were the Palaces* where Carlos Fuentes evokes the grandeur of houses and colonial palaces and where the city of my childhood, truer in fantasy than reality, became more tangible.

I lived my first fifteen years in close relationship with the stones and ghosts of the old city. When I took my first steps in it, Agustín Yáñez wrote *Ojerosa y Pintada*. In the novel, the driver does not act, strictly speaking, but his hearing records the voices of the city. Artists, beggars, prostitutes, workers, parading in the rolling window of the cab to form a talking mural of the fifties. When I was born, ten years before Efraín Huerta had published *Los Hombres del Alba* (Men of Dawn) the first book of poems dedicated completely to Mexico City. The panoramic painting of Juan O'Gorman where the capital appears viewed from the Monument to the Revolution is also from that time. It is the city that has moved beyond its traditional design, being quickly incorporated into the postwar economy. It is a smiling and peaceful city, a provincial city despite its conquests, and under whose facade stories that can only be generated in the universe of the city are unraveled. It is the city where Cantinflas' *Gran Hotel* premieres, but also one where the lost children of Huerta have "instead of a heart, a mad dog." It is still the city according to the human scale, but now with the beginning of the gigantism that lead to Salvador Novo exclaiming, "one gets, if you live in [the city] many years, to go only to a few places."

The child who one day, in this same space realized that there was a mystery called reading could not imagine that at the beginning of the next century he would find himself sharing those times in the city of the same name and, in spite of it being in a state of siege, in physical and moral decay, strangled by the rigors of pollution and the corruption of its inhabitants, it still allows these spaces where we, its children, dialogue with her to formulate declarations of hate and declarations of love, we try to decipher its signs, to seduce her before it destroys us.

The city was immense and intimate at the same time. We had nothing and we were not missing anything. The street was an endless territory, whose old buildings were our living present. The most real world was in black and white: matinees with triple showings in theaters with such hyperbolic names as their vast naves: Máximo, Colosal, Monumental. In them was born our unquenchable thirst for the horror that purifies: the one born on the other side of the screen and before which fortunately one can always close his eyes. And also our identification with a city that, lived daily, expressed itself on the screen in the first Cantinflas' movies, and those of Ismael Rodríguez and Alejandro Galindo.

Since my brothers and I had the use of reason, our house was occupied by books. They were also our brothers, although then we did not know it. Rather our step brothers. At the beginning, they received more pampering and care from my father than what he had for us. Some photographs of that remote era show the greatest luxury of our house on Allende Street, heart of the heart of Mexico City: the generous mahogany bookcase that housed the Balzac books beside the Justo Sierras, the Baudelaires next to the Carlos Pereyras that my father acquired with bibliomaniac and bibliophile passion. For him, a book was a significant and a meaning, a continent and a content. "An unbound book is not a book" he used to say with Vasconcelos, and devoted his meager saddler and teacher income to prettify his favorite children. Then came the time of the paternal fervor for the Reformation and the French Intervention: he concentrated on acquiring first editions about the great national decade, both in Mexican and foreign sources. Many of them came dressed in their original bindings; others, battered and heroic, entered as the liberal army, forged to the rhythm of the fight, and my father would take the task of restoring them with a love that compensated for his impatience. He would look for the best bookbinders, which are not always the cheapest. First among all was a craftsman whose last name was Ruiz, on Brazil Street, who gradually began to understand my father's style and taste. The bookbinder's work was cut short by the tyranny of alcohol that finally precipitated him to death.

My mother was the best ally of those books. Although they were even in the kitchen, she never protested against the invasion of those bastards. To top it off, my brothers and I increased their rows when we arrived home with new inhabitants after our excursions to the bookstores of Hidalgo Avenue: humble editions of Julio Verne and Arthur Conan Doyle on acid paper –better if they were used– and that we thought were treasures. We removed our original and humble musty smelling paperbacks and we became selective. We discovered in the Lomas de Chapultepec neighborhood a meritorious institution called Caza–Libros, whose funds were enriched with donations from American residents in Mexico. Due to such circumstances, the prices were more than moderate, and as teenagers we could get first editions of Henry James or one of Malcolm Lowry marked by his equally ethylic previous owner. Or that 1927 edition of Edgar Allan Poe, dedicated by successive people to their lucky owners.

When we moved to the Colonia Roma neighborhood, we did not have one but several libraries. Each of us carried his treasure, like the bones of the Amadises. As the house required major repairs and we had started high school, the parental authority decreed: "From today on, not even a pair of socks. But you can buy on credit all the books you want in Porrúa." That was the beginning of treatment and friendship with the young José Antonio Pérez Porrúa that, like all authentic booksellers, assisted his customers from behind the counter, like the rest of the infantry. Over the years, I realize that those visits when my friends seduced and oriented me with new books were the last vestige of the gatherings that made the bookstores sites of assembly and political gossip. Joaquín González Casanova was even more privileged: he had access to the hidden places where one could find bibliographic rarities. The tiger's children usually have more stripes than their father: if José Luis Martínez, bibliographer and greater bibliophile, was exemplary because of the order and maintenance of his books, his son Rodrigo is a more complete and finished version.

My father was capable of acquiring a book even if it was in a language he did not read, just because of its beauty. Thanks to such fervor, he was able to manage that the books dedicated to the death of Benito Juárez, in 1972, prepared by the Great Commission of the Chamber of Congress, were done in heavy paper, an austere but dignified binding and generous margins that make reading a double pleasure. The authors of such architecture and engineering were my friends Loera and Chávez, of noble publishing and book lineage.

It also happened that sometimes I would get to my room and, while looking for a book, it was not in its place. I had to go to my father's library to rescue it, sometimes with real boldness and without him noticing it. In revenge, he did the same, or he walked into my room to take stock of his own books that I had taken. Some of these temporary expropriations would become permanent. As all self–respected academic, he was a victim of second – hand booksellers. On one occasion he told the famous don Ubaldo López, head of a lineage even today, fortunately, in activity: "Now I cheated you. This book costs much more." Composed and smiling, don Ubaldo said, "So just one, don Martín, for all the other times that I have cheated you."

There is no bibliophile who does not complain of the great number of books that Gabriel Zaid says, not even the ones written but those for which one has the obligation to provide shelter, food and sustenance. The book is a rebellious creature and at the right time is affected by the Frankenstein syndrome. After my father's death came the earthquake of 1985. The area around our house was a complete devastation and we had to leave temporarily. The books became a burden, and although we did not confess it openly, my mother and my siblings got to think about donating them or selling them.

Fortunately, we were enlightened by the spirit of the Reformation and had the instinct to remember Melchor Ocampo. About to be shot by a conservative guerrilla at the Hacienda of Pomoca, he made his testament, which stipulated that his books should go to the college of San Nicolás Hidalgo, but that his selected friends could do a pre-screening to take the ones they liked the most. By mutual agreement, we have been doing the same with Martín Quirarte's library. A book, sooner or later, finds its rightful owner, and thus we have been distributing those books that annotated, bound and cared for by my father, reach new generations of readers, natural enemies of the book and lovers of photocopying and downloading information from the web. He was a happy man because he had the library that he had dreamed of from a young age, but also because he always knew how to share it. His students not only consulted the books in our house, but had the privilege of borrowing them. Especially the female students. When he died, the devotees and authentic tried to return them. Rogues, more intelligent, kept their inheritance. They are all reached by the conviction that the library of the happy man is, as the redeemed selfish giant of Oscar Wilde, one that makes us free, one which does not get mutilated when divided but thrives in others and retains the enthusiasm and love of its original owner.

Part of that library was donated to the National Library. Another one, more personal, I keep. I cure the scratches of those bratty kids, I take them to major healing when they cannot give one more step. Mateo González, head binder, now understands my phobias and my taste for guards and back labels that I prefer for each defenseless one. I leave his shop with them restored. I like to see them formed and bright, like hussars about to enter combat. Sometimes I despise them because they could not save their captain, because he did not know how to listen to them and win the battle in his concert. Fortunately, the tangible confirmation that they accompany me to decipher the double shame of the heroes, their unfinished face, the travelers as the discoverers of the territory closest to their soul, returns.

***

I was *Roman* from 1970, the year of the Soccer World Cup in Mexico and the premiere of the metro line that radically transformed the time and space between north and south. We moved to the Colonia Roma neighborhood, to an old house from the early twentieth century that Dad was responsible for remodeling. We arrived with forced happiness. Far from everything, we thought the down town —ours— was the only place to live, and we returned to it under any pretext, as I still do now, although many of my sites no longer recognize me. Gradually the house and the neighborhood were making us part of them until we realized that Colonia Roma was the only place to live. And to die. In El Ángel Funeral Home in Tonalá Street we have concentrated the tribal pain of successive departures.

If in the house on Allende Street our rites of childhood passage developed and our unbreakable passion for the city center was born, in the one on Zacatecas Street our ghosts and our own fearsome voices acquired full body. Our necessary metamorphosis. We call it, with surly tenderness, Usher House. Then it was called Poe

House to truly exorcize it. It had several renovations, some due to urgent need, and others by will. Dad never had the resources to fix it like he wanted, and the age of the house was felt in the late seventies when inclement rains caused the roof of the house to fall, precisely in the space where Dad worked. Concretely and symbolically the house sank, and with it its captain. Magda Solís, classmate in the Philosophy and Letters major, already married, with children who became my comrades, was, besides a great cook, a superb writer, a good witch and an unsurpassable Tarot reader. Without knowing exactly what was happening in my home and family environment, in one of her readings, the card that represented the Tower came for my present and my immediate future. Upside down. She explained what the particular symbolism meant for me. I transcribe her words more or less:

> This card represents the power of the consuming and purifying fire that destroys and sweeps out the old. The ego Tower staggers to its foundation. Everything we tried to keep is destroyed and the

supposed security of the past remains irrevocably shaken ... This knowledge of the true nature of the facts allows us to recognize the valuable gifts we receive through losses and painful disappointments. It symbolizes the relentless destruction that comes from heaven. It is an absolute healing energy; as it is necessary to remove from the body that which sickens it; just as the destruction of dead–end relations and situations that prevent development is required. All this can be very hostile, but relief automatically follows trauma.

The earthquakes of 1985 found us in our neighborhood, one of the hardest hit by the incessant Earth. I continued to be Roman, but I already lived on my own at the famous Casa de las Brujas in the Rio de Janeiro Plaza, which I had to abandon along with other victims, among others Guillermo Fernández who was never mourned enough. The family house held up a heroic trench amid the devastation. After Mom's death, we started an in depth remodeling of the house. We even added brand new sails to the boat with the captaincy of the architect Miguel del Río. We fortunately sold it to someone who produces movies and, therefore, will continue dreaming in it. Its ghosts left with us.

For twenty years I was a resident of Tlalpan. Returning from my stay as a professor in the United States in such a flat state where earthquakes are prohibited, I searched for a place to live that was settled in stone. The South, a fleetingly explored territory in my daily expeditions to Ciudad Universitaria, became a space where everything I needed to do was close by. Yet, for nine years I was a professor at the Autonomous Metropolitan University in Azcapotzalco. There are is a time for different kinds of madness. Getting to a seven o'clock class in the morning meant leaving home at half past five, with the stars still in the sky and when the streets were not set yet. These expeditions were prolonged reading days in the public transportation, which are now impossible. And in sudden acts of rebellion. Sometimes, instead of getting to the University, I got off the subway at the Hidalgo Station and would justify the lack of sense for my duties telling myself that I was practicing vagrancy as one of the fine arts by going down the streets of my first and definitive sentimental education. Such erring, that now I assume as a blessing and a necessary medicine, had its origin in one of the longest and most difficult visits I received from the Dark Lady and when I could not write anything because I could not think, although outwardly I labored to prove otherwise . That natural instinct of locomotion, as I have talked about it with my siblings, in which the body gets busy so that the soul does not defeat it, is one of the best obsessions that Dad left us.

When I was about to sleep, one of my childhood games was to imagine my bed like a boat across the sky that at the same time did not leave the room in which I slept. Then I did not know of the existence of a poet named Xavier Villaurrutia nor of his concept —learned in Paul Morand and earlier in Xavier de Meistre— that every trip is done first around the bedroom. Also, later I would learn of the similarity between my flying bed with the Spanish lullabies that were sung to tire the infant and put him to sleep. Like all children, lying on some patio I had the initiation of my metaphysical existence when I discovered the evidence of the rotation of the Earth.

My siblings and I did not miss a single issue of a comic book titled *Grandes Viajes*, where we learned the names and exploits of Marco Polo, Roald Amundsen and Charles Lindbergh. Among our favorite movies were *Twenty Thousand Leagues Under the Sea, Journey to the Center of the Earth* and *2001: A Space Odyssey*. Through downtown Mexico City, we began exhaustive strolls in an involuntary homage to the story *From the Apennine to the Andes* included in *Heart* by Edmondo de Amicis. An equally wonderful unforgettable reading was *The Wonderful Trip of Nils Holgersson through Sweden* by Selma Lagerlöf. Although the farthest trips we took were to Guadalajara, once aboard the Pullman we imagined that the train would be assaulted by Francisco Villa or Lawrence of Arabia, or that inside it we would live the intrigue of a story of Agatha Christie or Arthur Conan Doyle.

Writing is like this communion of the senses with the city that we discover and we make ours little by little. Reading as writing is a journey of the cultivated imagination, and even if we read in the line at the bank, formulate schemes as we train to withstand a marathon or decipher the darkness of an enigma in the midst of the loving battle, the words and actions of the others end up attaching themselves in the apparent stillness of the bedroom. Writing is traveling and traveling is reading and translating. I felt it, without knowing it when facing, also in my childhood, for the first time an essay without deciphering any of its mysteries. Just as there are people who do not deserve to travel, a bad word user will not know that he has traveled. Neo–Platonists read the Odyssey as a great allegory of the soul. Based on this requirement, it is necessary to undertake all movement: as definite as it can be to a man to go buy the newspapers, as useless to another to travel the world. The twenty – four hours of Leopold Bloom in Joyce's *Ulysses* teach us more than the passive hundred years of the one who chooses the cowardice of the sedentary over the imprudence of the vagabond. To read in the diverse realities of the world and to translate them to an objective language is like the reconstruction of the trip. And if trips, like the loves in your life, are ungrateful, the undertaken on behalf of the imagination and curiosity is the only reward from the platform. Thanks to the imagination we are allowed to travel without leaving our place and to see more places than permitted by displacement in space. Only the enamored reader gets first class tickets for the coach on that train.

Time has allowed me to know the world, feel its different geographies and understand that the traveler is a discoverer and a hero of himself: what his senses touch is born again with him, as if no one before him had seen it. Like the lover, he experiments in an astonishing short period a radical modification of his borders, both those that frame him in his every day and domestic space like those more subtle and enigmatic ones that delineate his body and soul. Everything is accelerated, everything is transformed. Everything is penetrated. The time of the trip makes of his protagonist a being suspended in the abyss. It does not matter if he is showed with illuminations or misadventures: the traveler is an eager page of signs, a sponge that absorbs what does not belong to him in principle and makes it his own, with an eagerness that not even the original inhabitants of that place have . Its time and space are those of the lover in the initial, unrepeatable moments of his passion, unrepeatable, of his absolute possession of the world.

There is a huge hotel called Earth. For a brief time in planetary dimensions, long in our parameters, we are privileged to be its guests until the natural ending of the biological cycle that tells us: it's time to exit. The check–out from this life is different for each of the occupants of our common lodging. Accomplices of the trip, hotels accompany us along our earthly adventure. In them we leave traces of memorable battles, of communion with the other, of individual angers and humiliations. To be alone in a hotel is to be alone with the world. Isolated from our habitual domesticity, the hotel confronts us with ourselves. Beyond the bedroom door, the personal odyssey begins or ends.

The traveling salesman in Hoper's painting who plays a solitary –the adjective was never used in a better way– in his hotel room. In a hotel, Anton Chekov died after wetting his lips in golden bubbles and exclaiming: "It has been long time since I have had champagne."

There is no individual anxiety similar to being in the hotel room that will live on for us for a few days, to open the window and to invite the city to enter the room. The almond trees in the Plaza de Armas invading the odorous gloom of Hotel Prendes in Veracruz; the colorful winter ducks from Central Park, defended from the winter by their beauty and framed by that window of the Hotel Saint Moritz; Monserrate emerging as a Chinese painting in the fog, almost within reach of my hand from the Hotel Tequendama in Bogota.

I guess I'll die a Southerner. Tlalpan, San Jerónimo, Olivar de los Padres, Cuicuilco and finally Tlacopac, San Ángel, have been the spaces of my last twenty–five years. Mexico City is an impossible place to live in, but it is the only place to live. Degraded, corrupted, dirty inside and out, dry and at the same time a victim of floods, besieges us and defeats us. It gives us unexpected rewards and victories. There are secrets and strategies to keep loving it: the renewed ceremony that means listening to the birds beginning the day despite our poisoned air; the cyclical children outside the schools; the sullen and distrustful multitude that, crammed on the subway, responds to our sneeze with a spontaneous and collective *bless you*; the cantina with a formica table waiting for the solitary drinker to face his benign and unforgiving mirror. Fortunately, there is a practice that does not leave me yet: the right to feel, as Carlos Valdés wrote, the street is still ours. I love my Tlacopac neighborhood as I love the woman who lives there, for whom I live. When I walk through it, when I touch it, I touch the body of the entire city, which has lived in me, for which I live.

VIII

La Invencible opens on Sundays. Its name comes from such provocation. Its resistance from such desecration. Its call is unconquerable for those coming to relieve the wounds of failure, deaf to the insistence of the bells in the nearby church of San Jacinto. The Invincible. Dilapidated and minimum its swing doors have renounced the threatened dignity of the glass. It seems as if born with San Ángel, where the deepest beats of the neighborhood converge, its institutions housed in buildings that conserve their original use and faces: the public bath whose brick facade reiterates its name, Colonial; the Melchor Múzquiz market where none of the colors, aromas, sounds of Mexico are missing; the San Jacinto Taxis site, that at 65 years of age holds the pride of being the oldest in the city.

La Invencible is flanked only by surnames, as if it had to do with school peers: Arteaga, Gálvez, Frontera. As you walk through the latter, it does not hurt to mention the complete name of General José Frontera, who transformed his civil status to confront the invader from the United States, was abandoned and died after the Padierna Battle: a plaque in San Jacinto, just recently placed, explains his memorable action. The names of the Irish Saint Patrick's Battalion were recorded before, commanded by John O'Reilly, some punished, others executed because they opposed a new conquest war. The annual ceremony that is organized every September 12 to remember them is so intimate that it is only known for the initiated and the inhabitants of the neighborhood: with their presence they pay homage to their ancestors who took down the bodies and gave them burial in the neighboring church of Tlacopac. It is reached by the street that preserves, in its majestic width, the name of Reyna. Other stories were not as mentioned but not because they were uncommon. One day in the nineteenth century, the young Manuel Payno came riding into San Ángel. In applying the adjective *sentimental* to his trip, he transformed the concept of practical locomotion into the pilgrimage of the soul. In the early twentieth century, the hard and youthful body of Santa passed, before boarding the train to a city where splendor and misery awaited her.

With its twenty square meters, La Invencible has the dimensions of a cabin. Its bar, the appearance of a pier where lost ships come to dock. In La Invencible you don't eat. Its tables accommodate at most four, but particularly invite the one alone. One drinks alone and one walks alone on the edge of life. And of death. Four resurrected ones share a black table with bottles, silent and humble and solemn owners each of their own loneliness, closer to the inexpressive absinthe drinkers of Degas than to the cheerful drunks of Velázquez.

La Invencible. The Spouter-Inn must have been like that, where *Moby Dick*'s Ishmael arrives, before beginning an adventure with unpredictable consequences. Life is not literature but its obligation is to be like it. Leviathan's harassment leads us to read the world and transform it into letters.

While I recover from the humiliating heat outside and gradually the body adapts to the freshness of this miraculous cave, I order a white

Herradura tequila accompanied by the coldest beer in the bar at that temperature that only the ice block knows how to create. A brother of Ishmael, named Bartleby, has come with me, inseparable companion since adolescence. In one of my lonely and long weekend walks, when the only unwavering thing was called reading, I had no choice but to stop on a bench to devour that inexhaustible text. Why bring Bartleby, to read it again, precisely today to La Invencible? Perhaps to convince myself that to add one more line to everything written is an impossible task, but there will always be other ways to say the same thing. Surely, when my father was advised to accept living a mutilated existence, with his eyes already somewhere else he said, "I 'd rather not:" in everything he did, he devoted himself to be faithful to this truth, based on stoic denial. He put his best cards on the written word. Not writing was dying.

La Invencible. The same adjective, also capitalized, was used by Felipe II to baptize his Armada. Each of its bronzes and sails, rigging and figureheads were invincible. The elements defeated it before its human enemies. Nothing defeats this other one.

That is the reason why the unprecedented power of the lower case prevails. Life is invincible and death is not; poetry is invincible, but there is no higher honor than facing it; invincible the amorous passion and its rough labyrinth of lures; invincible the Dark Lady of Melancholy, who spends long seasons at the home of those who leave their doors open.

Today is Sunday and I have passed my father's age when he decided to leave the world, unable to face the Invincible. Today I'm older than my father. Today my father is *the son that I don't have*. I believe I have some answers to the questions triggered by his premature, though not unexpected, departure. I have managed to conjure up the demons that at one point defeated him, but I find it impossible not to look at myself in his mirror. However, to be fair, "the grief of disquietude" has ceased to be. Born in a tired, remote and alien world, the lights are more abundant than the shadows. Restlessness and anxiety persist: without them, life would be an unworthy trade. Life is better than writing, but the blood stigma remains, for better and for worse, like the fire of Saint Telmo where the

Pequod harpooners tempered their weapons. To beat whiteness and silence, yes. To keep the honor, the manhood. To hold off the onslaught of the shadow. I do not want the Dad who bit his fists in anger against himself, instead of opposing them against the true adversary. I am seeking the authentic and creative insurrection, visible in the photograph of that young man who has left me in my mother's womb and on the other side of the Atlantic, in the middle of classes and his anxiety to see, to know and to feel, he has taken to the streets to take that picture, wrapped in a dark coat that refines his slenderness and challenges the winter of Madrid.

Rubén Bonifaz Nuño was born the same day and the same year that my biological father was born. In this neighborhood, the young Rubén dreamed of being a hero and magician. His deepest companions, called Salgari, Dumas and Rider Haggard, made him a reader. Even more, protagonist of battles where he put to practice the condition of the adventure with the announced risk of failure, supreme illumination of the one who takes risks. At 88, the same age that my father would be now, he fights every day for life, facing his daily humiliations with stoicism and courage and it makes us understand more and more the meaning of that verse of his which says that "it is worthier to suffer than being defeated." My father Martín stopped believing that when one writes for himself he is writing for someone else. And that other one, who perhaps we will never know, justifies us without knowing it. My father Rubén's poem involves writing for those that, despite their helplessness, and thanks to their helplessness, forge their weapons to maintain the ignored heroism of being a man.

After the starting gun in the long distance races, the main stimulus is the phrase "we will wait for you all at the goal." When those of us who have a mediocre performance, reach the half way mark of the competition, it is an honor to see the leaders, Kenyans with antelope legs, surrounded by scarcities and double will to defeat them. We know they will get there before everyone else. One keeps running, convinced of not having the body, the condition, the discipline of the one that is heading that eager and free group of us to which we devote every minute and effort of that day. When glimpsing the goal and crossing it with the last breath, we are part of the hero who did the same as us but did it better. It is the same thing with writing. Writing is to have pride and humility. In that order. Pride to predict, as Zola: "I will be Balzac or nothing." Humility to admire the glory of the one who has seen what we have thought we saw. One crosses the finish line as one can and not as one should. It is not a lack of effort, but full awareness of the powers available to us. It is possible to expand them, to train them, but we know intimately what we are. The expression *we will wait for you all at the goal* may be a sister to the bitter and arrogant phrase of Salieri when he tells his confessor; "Welcome to the world of mediocrity." in its deepest sense, it underlines the ancestral wisdom rescued by one of our younger classics:

> A muleteer once told me
> that you don't have to be first,
> but you have to know how to get there.

October 1993. Not one woman hurts through all my body, as in the verse that Borges dedicates to the wounded. It hurts up to my last muscle after subjecting them through the effort of the half marathon. Running is like writing. Not doing it would end that inexplicable and absurd suffering. But it would also end the most sublime and full enjoyment achieved in solitude. Another piece of Flaubert bathes me with the same vigor and strength of the shower that baptizes me as if it was the first time: "But life is so short. I will never write what I want, not even one fourth of what I dream. All this force that you feel and suffocates you, will have to die without overflowing it. "

You arrive at La Invencible with questions. You never leave with answers. The first tequila horse neighing on the empty stomach brightens up even the last of the stones in the neighborhood. A rain which seems like it will last, falls on the neighborhood and gives us the momentary illusion that, just like stones it seems like they are going to keep this brief shine eternally, the distance between experience and writing will be shorter. So that the fire born of the impact can be the fruit of the substance and not of the artifice. To distance the words of life so they come closer to it.

Like many other reoffending images, I rekindle one of the last days we lived in downtown before moving to the Colonia Roma neighborhood, land back then unknown and promised. Dad is inside the only car he had. While the young man who drove for him arrives, he waits, reading as always. A parishioner of La Antigua Roma, out of a movie of Ismael Rodríguez, comes close, curious and insolent. With her fermented breath, she asks him a question that is an affirmation of discovering a being apparently alien to the neighborhood. "Hey, my guardian, what's up?" My father looks at her and spontaneously laughs childishly in a laugh that probably never left him. He laughs not at the woman, but with her: he mocks himself. I hang onto that gesture so that he does not abandon me.

In his last class, Professor Quirarte left only one assignment. With the passing of time, I have learned that it was to write the letter that he could not leave us. His legacy was life, the invincible. His final act has led us to try to exhaust it, spread its legs, seduce it relentlessly to achieve its highest gifts. Like writing, it can be conquered at times, as long as we are worthy of the weapons to combat it, making it our ally and defeat the common enemy. The day Dad died I began my task in a different way. I haven't finished it yet in these many years that are too many already. If to live is to write with the whole body, resistance is better that existence.

Tlacopac, San Angelo,
January 2010–June 2012.

INDEX

Vicente Quirarte

About the Author

Vicente Quirarte (Mexico City, 1954) holds a PhD in Mexican Literature from the Department of Philosophy and Letters of the National Autonomous University of Mexico, where he is a professor as well as a researcher at the Institute of Bibliographic Research of the same institution. He is a member of the Mexican Academy of Language and the National College.

His work includes books of poetry, narrative, theater, literary criticism and historical essay. His essay work has gone through different directions. He has done studies of Mexican poetry as *Peces del aire altísimo* or *El azogue y la granada*. One of the lines of study he has developed in recent years is the analysis of travel literature written by Mexicans, such as *Jerusalén a la vista. Tres viajeros mexicanos en Tierra Santa; Más allá de la visión de Anáhuac. Poética de los viajeros mexicanos,* and *Republicanos en otro imperio. Viajeros mexicanos a Nueva York 1830–1895.* His systematic study of Mexico City seen by writers appears in the book *Elogio de la calle.*

Biografía literaria de la Ciudad de México (1850–1992), as well as the essays collected under the title *Amor de ciudad grande*. His works on poetry include *La poética del hombre dividido en la obra de Luis Cernuda, El azogue y la granada, Peces del aire altísimo, Invitación a Gilberto Owen, El México de los Contemporáneos*. His most recent collection of poems is called *La miel de los felices*.

He has received the Xavier Villaurrutia Award, the Sergio Magaña Dramaturgy Prize, the Ibero–American Poetry Award "Ramón López Velarde" and the National University Prize.

About the Translator

Elvia Ardalani (H. Matamoros, Mexico, 1963) is a Professor of Spanish and Creative Writing in the Department of Writing and Language Studies at the University of Texas–Rio Grande Valley. Her work has appeared in different anthologies in the United States, Mexico and Spain. She has published the following poetry books: *El ser de los enseres, Callejón Kashaní, Cuadernos para un huérfano, Miércoles de Ceniza, De cruz y media luna/From Cross and Crescent Moon, Y comerás del pan sentado junto al fuego*, and Por *recuerdos viejos, por esos recuerdos*. She co–edited the volume *Miguel Hernández desde América* published by the Fundación Cultural Miguel Hernández in Orihuela, Spain and The University of Texas–Pan American Press. She has translated to Spanish and English the poetry of Jalal al–Din Rumi, Omar Khayam, Elizabeth Bishop and others, as well as the works of some contemporary poets like Armando Alanís Pulido, Héctor Carreto, Vicente Quirarte and René

Rodríguez Soriano. Her first novel, *El sótano del caracol*, is in the process of publication.

Other **Poetry Books** in Libros Medio Siglo